Sex and the

Single Mom

D1565594

Sex and the Single Mom

THE ESSENTIAL GUIDE TO DATING, MATING, AND RELATING

Sharon McKenna

TEN SPEED PRESS
Berkeley | Toronto

Ten Speed Press
Box 7123 • Berkeley, California 94707 • www.tenspeed.com

Distributed in Australia by Simon and Schuster Australia, in Canada by Ten Speed Press Canada, in New Zealand by Southern Publishers Group, in South Africa by Real Books, and in the United Kingdom and Europe by Airlift Book Company.

Cover and text design by Toni Tajima

Library of Congress Cataloging-in-Publication Data
McKenna, Sharon.
    Sex and the single mom : the essential guide to dating, mating, and relating / Sharon McKenna.
        p. cm.
    Summary: "An intelligent and lighthearted guide to navigating the dating world as a single mother"—Provided by publisher.
    Includes index.
    ISBN-13: 978-1-58008-744-5
    ISBN-10: 1-58008-744-2
    1. Single mothers—Social life and customs. 2. Single mothers--Sexual behavior. 3. Dating (Social customs) I. Title.
    HQ759.915.M42 2006
    646.7'7086947—dc22   2005035598

Printed in the United States of America
First printing, 2006

1 2 3 4 5 6 7 8 9 10 — 10 09 08 07 06

NEW LEAF PAPER
ENVIRONMENTAL BENEFITS STATEMENT

Sex and the Single Mom is printed on New Leaf Ecobook 50, made with 100% recycled fiber, 50% post-consumer waste, processed chlorine free. By using this environmental paper, Ten Speed Press saved the following resources:

trees	water	energy	solid waste	greenhouse gases
12 fully grown	4,252 gallons	8 million BTUs	554 pounds	951 pounds

Calculated based on research done by Environmental Defense and other members of the Paper Task Force.
©2006 New Leaf Paper   www.newleafpaper.com   888.989.5323

FOR SINGLE MOTHERS EVERYWHERE

contents

acknowledgments

The fact that I managed to write this book while also raising a family on my own and earning a steady paycheck still astounds me. Writing takes energy, of which I have so little; it takes patience, most of which is expended on my children; and it takes time, which is in seriously short supply in my life. So how did I do it? I called in reinforcements and I drank a lot of coffee. And I was lucky enough to have children who think that writing a book is a pretty cool thing to do, so they actually left me alone for a few minutes here and there to work. So first and foremost I'd like to give an extra-special thanks to my sons, Kieran and Declan. The royalties will go straight into your college fund, I promise. Many thanks to Cory, the best ex a girl could ever have, for giving me a break when I needed it (which was a lot); to Jason, for missing his plane and thereby changing my life; and to a few lesser men out there who, by showing me how bad a boyfriend can be, inspired me to expect, and get, only the very, very best.

I'm very grateful to my agent, June Clark, and feel fortunate to have her in my corner. Thanks also to my editor, the always perceptive and eternally patient Julie Bennett. You'll make a great mom someday.

Finally, I'd like to thank the moms, single and otherwise, who have inspired and supported me throughout the years: Carla, Vicki, Megan, Karen, Maggie, Dominique and, most of all, my own mother, Betty McKenna. Your strength and love lives on in me and my children, always.

foreword

Single motherhood is a life passage like no other. It's a wild and wondrous, rocking and rolling journey whose challenges are immense and gifts extraordinary. Single moms want love, sex, and companionship of the adult variety—just like every other woman out there. And while being a single mom does make dating more difficult sometimes, it absolutely does *not* mean we are doomed to a life alone.

I have received thousands of letters from single mothers since the publication of my book *The Single Mother's Survival Guide*. Women of every age, race, religion, and circumstance have shared their amazing and heartfelt stories. Despite the differences in each woman's situation, the letters have a prevailing theme: It is the loneliness that is hardest to bear. Beyond the exhausting financial and physical struggles of being a single mother, we all ache for another adult to share our life—and our bed—with.

About a year or so ago I received a friendly email from one of my readers, a single mom named Sharon McKenna. Sharon told me that she was writing a book about the challenges of dating while raising a family alone and she wanted to brainstorm about single motherhood, the publishing business, and the best ways to reach the millions of single mothers out there. We spent a short time chatting—after all, as single mothers, neither of us had much time to spend on the phone—and I wished Sharon luck on her book. Because the number of people who tell me they are writing a book is staggeringly higher than the number of people who actually do it, I was shocked and excited when Sharon called to say that the book was done, and would I be willing to write a foreword?

Way to go, Sharon! You bet I'll write a foreword. Single mothers need books written just for them. And when it comes to sex, love, and romance, I can tell you from experience that there are few (if any) books that address the single motherhood perspective. Sharon tells it like it is (and then some). This book made me laugh out loud at the hilarity, and sometimes the sheer absurdity, of our love life situations. She holds nothing back—and that's my kinda gal. As I read *Sex and the Single Mom*, I thought back to the thirteen years I spent as a mom without a steady boyfriend. I remember that it felt impossible to fit even one date into my week.

The challenge (and joy) of dating as a single mom is something that only another single mom can understand. This book is a wonderfully complete, honest, and user-friendly guide for any woman walking the wild and jagged path of single motherhood. Sharon's advice is helpful, insightful, and written with the warmth of a best friend. I wish it had been around when I was struggling with my own dating life—it would have been a welcome comfort. I invite you to curl up on the couch with this book and start the ball rolling in your love life again. And remember that in the eyes of your children and all the sisters who have been where you are . . . you're a hero and you deserve this. Happy hunting, ladies.

—Patrice Karst, author of *The Single Mother's Survival Guide*, *The Invisible String*, and *God Made Easy*

Introduction

HAVEN'T WE MET SOMEWHERE BEFORE?

I know book introductions are supposed to be the place where the author shares her life story and rattles on about how, why, and where the book came to be. For the most part, however, this isn't one of those introductions, because *Sex and the Single Mom* isn't about me.

It's about you.

You know who you are. You're the friendly young woman I used to run into at that funky clothing store in Venice Beach, the one who'd notice my bulging belly and want to know when I was due and whether the baby's father was excited. And when I told you that there wasn't one—a dad, that is—your face lit up. You said how cool it was that I was going it alone and that someday, if you didn't meet a great guy, you'd be doing the same thing. I've met many women who made similar predictions, and it looks like a lot of you meant what you said because single women are choosing to have children on their own through donor insemination, adoption, or other means in record numbers.

Or you might be one of those moms that I'd run into at the park, married but miserable, envious of my freedom but fright-

1

ened to death that you'd end up in my situation. Well, guess what? Many of you are divorced single moms, even though you thought you never would be, and now you're wondering if you'll ever experience love and lust again. (You will, trust me.)

Or maybe you are one of the many single moms I met in person or corresponded with while I wrote this book. You told me your stories, many of which made me laugh, and an equal number of which made me sad, because it was clear you're smart, funny, hip, interesting women with a lot of love to give, and you're having a tough time finding any takers. In fact, you're not sure *how* to love again, or even if you want to, given what you've been through in the past. You might be confused or ambivalent about trying to date while raising your children; though, many of you are also enthusiastic about the possibilities for your love life. And all of you are looking for help, a few laughs, and someone to commiserate with.

That's exactly what I was looking for when I was ready to date again, yet no matter how hard I looked, I couldn't find a book or seminar or website or even other single mothers to help me figure out how to date now that I was a mom. I complained about this endlessly until a friend said (just to shut me up, I'm sure), "You're a writer. Go write a book about it."

Four years later, here we are. And while there are now many more resources for single moms than there were back then, I believe this is the first book that *realistically* and *holistically* tackles the issues surrounding sex and single motherhood—and it does so with a sense of humor. I wanted to write a book that was up-to-date, a bit in your face, and, above all, honest, because the single moms I know aren't interested in sugarcoating their situation. They want it straight, they want solutions, and they want to be spoken to in a manner that reflects the bright, funny, and sexy women they know they are.

But before you read further, I feel obligated to tell you what this book can—and can't—do for you, and why reading it will absolutely, positively change your perspective on single motherhood and relationships. *Sex and the Single Mom* is as much about how to *not date* (or how to deal with the fact that you can't find a date or that you don't feel ready for romance) as it is about how to find a great guy. Because, let's face it, there will be dry spells, and it's important that you understand how to handle those stretches in between boyfriends or lovers in a healthy way.

This book is also about empowerment and self-esteem, with a little bit of politics and sociology thrown in. In other words, it's the guide to single motherhood and dating for the thinking, feeling woman who has a healthy sense of humor and a healthy libido.

This book is also more about you—your self-image, your needs, your body, your angst—than it is about your children and how your love life impacts them (although I do address the latter in Chapter Six). It is important to consider your kids, of course, but I wanted this book to address *you*, a single woman with romantic and sexual wants and needs. So much of your life is centered on your kids; I felt it was important to focus on you.

I have dated, had serious relationships (and a few flings), and developed some great friendships since I became a parent. I started out naïve and unprepared for how my life would change when I became a single mom, but I ended up stronger, happier, and more fulfilled than I've ever been. In between were some mighty dark days, a few broken hearts, and a lot of growth. I want you to learn from my experiences, both good and bad, and from the experiences of other single moms across the country. They have some great advice to give and funny stories to tell, and I'm grateful for their contributions. (By the way, I've written the book from the perspective of a heterosexual woman, which I am, but I've spoken with gay single mothers as well, and they struggle with many of the same issues as the hetero moms I heard from. The advice contained here applies to us all.)

I believe that single moms deserve to go out into the trenches of sex and relationships armed with real insights and the strength necessary to create a genuinely happy and fulfilling love life. I also believe there is no one quick fix for your dating and relationship dilemmas. In this book I've taken a broad approach to getting your love life on track to help you create a solid foundation on which to build your own little love shack.

I hope *Sex and the Single Mom* helps you to do just that—and then some. And it will, if you simply open your mind, your heart, and, most of all, your eyes.

chapter one

The Single Mother Myth

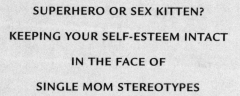

SUPERHERO OR SEX KITTEN?

KEEPING YOUR SELF-ESTEEM INTACT

IN THE FACE OF

SINGLE MOM STEREOTYPES

*"I'm not just some slut
you can bang a couple of times and
throw in the garbage."*
—Glenn Close as Alex Forrest in *Fatal Attraction*

*"Self-esteem and self-contempt have
specific odors; they can be smelled."*
—Eric Hoffer (1902–83), philosopher and author of
The Passionate State of Mind

Who are you, anyway? Are you the sexpot home wrecker, chasing after your best friend's husband? Or maybe the embittered, lonely divorcée who has vowed never to love again? Perhaps you're the trailer-livin', trash-talkin' single mom who pops out children like a kitten has litters. And then again, you could be that most modern of single moms—the one who is married to her job, selfishly ignores her children, and has traded in the rewards of relationships to slave at the altar of success.

These are but a handful of the single mom stereotypes that endure today, despite the fact that single mothers are no more slutty, stupid, or obsessed with success than their childless or married female counterparts. So why do society, the media, and politicians insist on slapping us with these unfortunate labels? Perhaps it's because we don't conform to any familiar image: we aren't Harriet, the 1950s housewife of *The Adventures of Ozzie and Harriet*, nor are we the freewheeling single girls of *Sex and the City*, and we are nothing like the over-the-hill spinster aunt we remember from our childhood.

The media, conservative politicians, and other assorted opinion-makers will no doubt continue to foster inaccurate images of the single mother. The good news, however, is that there is a new trend toward acknowledging what we've known all along: that single moms are heroes rather than home wreckers; strong and independent rather than needy and desperate; and hardworking and successful, but not at the expense of their children.

Indeed, after being kicked around for years (well, actually, for forever), single moms—with their increasing influence in every arena, from entertainment to politics to consumer spending—are fast becoming the hot demographic du jour. As evidence, note that the Internet powerhouse Yahoo!, which has one of the most highly trafficked personals websites, launched "Single Mom's Month" in May 2005, offering moms one month's free use of their personals section. This highly visible effort to single out single moms, along with a number of other important developments we will discuss in the last chapter, signals a sea change in how the single mother demographic is starting to be seen. Corporate America is smart enough to understand the massive spending power of single moms, who now number an estimated ten million in the United States alone according to the U.S. Census Bureau, although many experts believe the actual number is much higher, perhaps even double that estimate. And our ranks continue to grow, as the number of births to unmarried women increases every year. Adoptions and donor inseminations rates are also on the rise. In fact, single parent–headed households are now the fastest-growing family type worldwide.

But just because we are finally getting the attention we deserve, that doesn't mean it's always the kind of notice we want or that a majority of people understand us any better than they ever did.

> *"I have been treated like a second-class citizen due to being a single mom. People look down on single mothers and are not willing to help with simple things like holding a door open or picking up something that I had dropped because my hands were already full. I recall holding my baby while on a crowded bus where no one gave up their seat for me, even when I asked. Faces turned away from me as though I were diseased."*
>
> —Jasmine, 43, Toronto

In an academic essay entitled "Oh Baby! Representations of Single Mothers in American Popular Culture" published in *Americana: The Journal of American Popular Culture*, Austin College professor of English Robin Silbergleid writes that "[narrative] representations of mothers, fathers and families do a great deal of ideological work. They can, as Dan Quayle has done, depict single mothers as selfish home wreckers, or as *Marie Claire* has done, everyday heroes. Either way, such representations have little to do with the practical realities of single-parent families in the United States." She refers, of course, to that defining moment in the evolution of single motherhood, an episode of the 1980s television show *Murphy Brown* in which the main character, Murphy, decides to have a child on her own. This fictional TV episode made Vice President Dan Quayle positively apoplectic. In his infamous 1992 speech, Quayle whined about our troubled society, saying that "It doesn't help matters when primetime TV has Murphy Brown, a character who supposedly epitomizes today's intelligent, highly paid professional woman, mocking the importance of fathers by bearing a child alone and calling it just another lifestyle choice." A firestorm of controversy followed his remarks, and suddenly single moms were thrust into a very harsh spotlight that has dimmed only slightly in the years since.

We haven't heard much from Mr. Quayle since then—thank goodness—and the Murphy Brown brouhaha is now more than two decades old, but the tendency to crucify single moms who are openly independent lingers on.

"I knew when I had Nicholas that there would be financial hardships. And I am a woman with a lot of pride. So the day I walked into the welfare office was a pretty shameful day for me. All I wanted was some sort of child-care voucher or assistance so I could stay in school (I was enrolled at a four-year college studying English and Secondary Ed) and work full-time to pay the bills. The woman showed no mercy listening to my story. I explained how I didn't want to stay on welfare, how I just needed a boost for a couple of months to get on my own two feet. She made remarks about how my baby's father should be the one contributing, not the state. And this is woman-to-woman mind you. She even went so far as to say I shouldn't stay in school, I should just work full-time or go to beauty school. Beauty school?! I was planning to be a high

school teacher! It had been my dream all my life! And give it up for beauty school?! I left the office crying, and over the course of several months tried to go back to receive that voucher. I never did."

—Julie, 21, Boston

Mirror, Mirror on the Wall

So what does all of this have to do with you and sex, dating, and relationships?

Like it or not, how the world sees you can play a big part in how you see yourself. And how you see yourself plays a huge part in how successful your love life will be. You can't control how a man will perceive you once he knows you're a single parent, but you can control how you view yourself and how you project that perception into the world.

WHAT'S IN A NAME?

We are a nation of labelers. We like to group people into neat little categories and assign all sorts of descriptive terms to them. We don't simply talk about "families" anymore; instead there are "two-parent households" and "single-parent households." Adolescents are now classified as "generation Y" or "tweens." People no longer dwell in cities or the suburbs; they are now "urbanites" or "exurbanites." Consumer marketing is behind much of the labeling, but so are political and social agendas. Sometimes a label comes with benefits. I personally believe it's mostly a good thing that the categories "single mom" and "single parent" are finally coming into their own and that these groups are starting to throw their weight around a bit.

"I think the desperate single mom stereotype has been heavily eroded," notes relationship expert and author Dr. Pepper Schwartz. "Twenty years ago when you said 'single mom,' you thought welfare mother or pregnant teenager. Now it includes anyone who has been hit by the high divorce rate."

Still, when used in a more intimate setting, and particularly in some social situations, the label "single mom" can be unbelievably irritating. Take, for example, the time I went to a party with a younger, prettier female friend. My twins were only a few months old at the time, and I hadn't been out of the house in weeks except to buy diapers or formula or to drive the boys around the block until they fell asleep. So on this night, I went out of my way to look good. I was excited to be a woman again and, for a few hours at least, leave the mom in me at home.

We had been at the party less than ten minutes when a gorgeous guy walked up. He made small talk with my friend, but he was looking at me. Just as I was about to introduce myself, my friend announced, "This is my friend Sharon. She's a single mom."

I will never forget that moment. It was the first time my first name had been attached to something other than my last name. This new label startled me and, as I think my slightly jealous friend had intended, it also spooked the good-looking guy.

In an instant, I went from being just "Sharon" to being a whole host of other things: an easy lay (bad); a strong, independent woman (good); and a depressed, lonely woman looking for love (really bad, even if at the time there was some truth to that one). I considered running for the door when the guy said with a genuine smile, "Wow! That's great." My friend skulked off to find easier prey, and the hottest guy at the party and I talked most of the night. We ended up having a nice little romance for a few weeks.

So the next time someone makes it a point to mention that you're a single parent in a situation where it has absolutely no relevance, you might try tossing a few labels their way. For instance, I could have easily introduced my friend by saying, "This is my friend Carly. She'll screw anything." (Many names in this book have been changed to protect the innocent—and the very, very guilty.) Or when a self-satisfied married couple introduces you as their "single mom friend," as if you're a visitor from some faraway and slightly scary third world nation, consider introducing them like this: "These are my married friends Sam and Sheila. They haven't had sex for over a year." Or, better yet, let's ditch the labels altogether and try something really radical: introducing people by their names only and leaving the labels out of it.

Happily, a recent study suggests that single moms may feel a lot better about themselves than one might expect, given the way they are often portrayed. In particular, this research found that single mothers had better self-esteem and "sex esteem" than single childless women in the same study.

The research was conducted on behalf of True (www.true. com), an online relationship service, by Karin Bruckner, licensed therapist and single parent expert, and James Houran, Ph.D., True's director of psychological studies. Using data from extensive personal profiles True members must complete when they join the service, the team compared responses from thirty thousand women, and what they found astounded them.

"We looked at areas like sexuality, parenting-engendered traits, how they handle conflict, emotional IQ kinds of skills," said Houran. Across the board, single mothers scored higher in terms of sexual attitudes and behavior and in what the researchers refer to as "parent-engendered" qualities such as selflessness, flexibility, and practicality.

"I was surprised," said Bruckner. "I'm a single mom myself and I was surprised. But it makes sense. I think, overall, what we can say is that single parents have all the benefits of parenting children, all the benefits that brings in terms of maturity and wisdom and self-development, because you truly have to rise to the occasion as a single parent. So what they lack in terms of freedom, lifestyle, or resources they certainly make up for—and more." In other words, all the hard work and stress single moms experience while parenting, and all the patience and negotiating skills they are required to develop, can pay extra dividends by making them better equipped to have a successful relationship.

According to the same study, another payoff happens between the sheets. Single mothers scored as high or higher than single women on measures of libido and sexual attitudes. "Being a single parent makes you more giving in a lot of ways, and that's expressed in another way in the bedroom," explains Houran. "And you're more open-minded—not so judgmental."

Bruckner adds, "I think their sexuality is so much deepened by their experience of maintaining a family life and the commitment and selflessness that it takes to do that. It's all tied together."

Yet, as many of us single moms know, squeezing in time for sleep, let alone sex, can be difficult. But here, too, single moms have an advantage over the merely single, according to Houran. "If you want to have sex [as a single parent] you have to be more adaptable," he believes. "When we first published our press release, people were very interested, because it did fly in the face of what people would generally think, especially when it comes to sexuality."

Dr. Schwartz believes the very fact that single moms have children can perhaps contribute to having a better sex life. "In the best of all possible worlds, in a marriage you have a great partner *and* a great sex life. But this isn't true for a lot of marriages. There is either habituation or anger that undercuts things," she notes. "If you're a single mom, you might not have the best of it, but you don't have the worst of it either. So when you're single, and you're getting love and support on one level from your children, you can get your emotional base there and your sexual base elsewhere."

Although the True study revealed some very uplifting data about single moms and self-esteem, it also indicated that single mothers don't always utilize all their advantages when it comes to dating and relationships. In a press release announcing the results of the study, Brucker noted, "The challenge is that there is not a lot of recognition of the wonderful character traits they possess. In fact, many single mothers subscribe to society's rather negative views of themselves instead of accessing the highly developed attributes they possess."

NAUGHTY AND NICE SELF-ESTEEM BOOSTERS

- Limit the amount of time you spend with married couples—unless they are totally miserable with each other, in which case being around them will make you feel really, really good about being single.

- Focus on your kids. Nothing can make you more proud of yourself than your ability to raise great children.

- Have a fling with a much, much younger guy. If he has six-pack abs and a supertight tush, that's even better. Men use arm candy all the time in order to feel better about themselves, so why shouldn't we?

- Watch what you watch. TV is notorious for creating caricatures of single moms. Turn off the over-the-top reality TV and turn on the History Channel. Better yet, read a book—this one, for starters!

- Come out of the closet. While you don't want to wear your status as a single mom on your sleeve, you shouldn't hide it either. It can be very empowering to let people know you're doing it all on your own. They'll pay you compliments, some of them even genuine, which you should repeat to yourself every night, like a mantra, just before you fall asleep.

- Do things by yourself. Go to the movies, a street fair—even a restaurant—all by your little lonesome. At first this will feel strange and scary, and perhaps you'll even think everyone is staring at you and whispering about what a loser you are (they're not, by the way). After a while, though, you will begin to feel supremely self-confident because you'll realize you can go out and enjoy life without a man by your side.

- **Run or walk a marathon.** The sense of accomplishment you'll gain by finishing it and the pounds you'll lose while preparing for it are a confidence-building combo that's hard to beat.

- **Flirt profusely.** The instant buzz you get from getting someone else's attention, whether it's with a witty comeback or a low-cut blouse, can do wonders for your self-image.

Assuming you're reading this book because you want to have a successful love life, you need to be honest with yourself about your self-esteem. Do you like yourself? Do you have a fulfilling home life? Is your career satisfying? Are you over the wounds of your last breakup or divorce? Do you have the energy to invest in a relationship, given that you are the sole parent? In other words, are you "relationship material"? Or are you so frazzled or angry or full of self-loathing that you can actually relate to the psychotic single-mom-to-be in the movie *Fatal Attraction*?

Look, we all have some areas that need improvement. Everyone is a work in progress all their lives. But if you want to get the dating thing right this time, you need to start from a place of solid self-esteem and confidence. If you're not there, find a good therapist or support group and take the time necessary to get yourself there. Trust me, it'll be worth it. Men, sex, and relationships have been around since Adam and Eve did that thing with the apple. They aren't going anywhere. Besides, the right romantic situation simply won't come along until you're feeling good about yourself and your life.

If you believe you're ready to take what the dating world has to dish out, read on and find out how to jump-start your love life. But if you have some doubts, listen to your inner voice and give romance a rest for now while you work on *you*. Your children, your future lovers, and, most of all, *you* will be glad you did.

"I was never angry at men—disappointed, maybe, but not angry— rather, I became very angry about a society that deems only the 'traditional' family normal and which pretty much tells single moms, 'Screw you. Want to stay home with your baby? Too bad. We'll leave you to navigate the complicated, expensive, and really inconsistent world of child care alone and all but force you to put your infant in daycare despite our constant repetition that small children should stay home with their mothers. We won't offer any assistance without requiring that you be destitute first, and then only with a heaping helping of humiliation.' Two-parent families are offered all kinds of moral and intellectual support, but single parents are told that their families are dysfunctional and damaging (as if two-parent families are guaranteed to be good ones!)."

—Carrie, 37, Boston

The Sisters Are Doing It for Themselves

Clearly, it's been a long, rough road for single moms. While struggling to raise our children we've had to endure everything from outright hostility to more subtle forms of discrimination. So does that mean we go around feeling sorry for ourselves? No way. First of all, who has the time for self-pity? And at any rate, by providing us with such a meager support system, society has forced us to become more self-reliant and self-confident. Ironically, the very attempts to keep us down have succeeded in inspiring our drive to do well, as parents, partners, workers, and friends.

So here's the bottom line: there's more to creating a fulfilling love life than surfing the online personal ads and going out on blind dates. It starts with the belief that you are a catch. Once you believe that with all your heart, you're ready to go fishing (or, better yet, shopping) for romance.

chapter two

Shopping for Love

BEFORE YOU PUT YOURSELF

OUT THERE, MAKE SURE YOU KNOW WHAT

YOU'RE IN THE MARKET FOR

"I base my fashion taste on what doesn't itch."
—Gilda Radner

*"The great question that has never been answered and
which I have not been able to answer,
despite my thirty years of research into the feminine soul,
is, what does a woman want?"*
—Sigmund Freud

I t's perfectly natural to believe that a partner will make your life better. That's why so many single moms embark on the dating journey with the hope of landing a solid, long-term relationship the first time they dip their toe into the choppy waters of the dating world. What many of us fail to do is to ask ourselves if we're really in a position to dedicate the time and energy necessary to make a committed relationship succeed, or if, in fact, that's what we want at all. Newly divorced moms in particular are often torn between relishing their newfound freedom and a desire to fill that cold, empty place on the other side of the bed with something other than the family dog.

If you're a single mom who wants to enter the romantic marketplace and come away completely satisfied, the good news is that you already have the skills you need to get what you want. It's called being a smart shopper. Many of us are natural-born shoppers, but it's the "smart" part that most of us need work on.

Land of the Spree

Sometimes we go shopping and just pick up whatever strikes our fancy, but for important purchases, such as the perfect little black dress that will make you the envy of the holiday party, we invest much more time. We scour the malls. We surf the best shopping sites. We buy fashion magazines to check the latest fashion trends. We try on many, many cocktail dresses.

When you're shopping for love, I advocate adopting a strategy much like the quest for the perfect little black dress, especially when you're just beginning your search. Later, when you have a pretty firm grasp on what does and does not work for you, going on a shopping spree without any thought about what you might be, um, taking home, is just fine. Once you're an experienced shopper, it's okay if you end up with something you wish you'd never picked up in the first place and rush to return it the next day. It's perfectly fine if you stumble across something you're crazy about for a few weeks, until you're sick and tired of it and you give it the toss.

If you're a novice, however, a careless approach might make you so skittish you vow never to go shopping for love again, so I suggest taking a good hard look inside your own mental and emotional closet before you even *look* at any merchandise.

Size Matters. What's Yours?

How many times have you looked back at the romantic choices you've made in the past and cringed? Recalling the ghosts of boyfriends past can be a painful, embarrassing process, but it's one that I highly recommend you torture yourself with before you start your search for love as a single mom. Why? Because it makes you realize, in the most painful way, that what felt right for you in years past may be totally wrong for you now. Now that you have children, you need to more closely scrutinize any potential mate. You don't want to look back at this time in your life as one in which you made even more bad romantic choices. Those mistakes will look even worse when you realize you made them as a mom—in other words, you'll know you *should have known better*. So, when it comes to finding a boyfriend in "your size" (I'm speaking metaphorically, of course), you need to be ruthlessly realistic about what size *you* are. Just like when we go shopping for clothes, we may think we're still a size eight when we're actually a ten or a twelve. Why not avoid the frustration of trying to squeeze yourself into something that does-n't fit? It's depressing and a total waste of time.

Getting a good idea about what kind of man will fit your life now requires that you do an inventory of how you've grown since you were last seriously involved—and I'm not talking about those extra pounds on your hips and thighs. Your mental and physical health, sexual needs and desires, and life goals have no doubt changed since you became a parent. We'll explore all of these areas in more detail in subsequent chapters, but for now, take some time to size up your life. When you do, it will become obvious what types of men will be a good fit and what types you shouldn't even consider trying on.

What Shape Are You In?

As any woman who has ever stood before a three-way mirror while trying on bathing suits clearly understands, even the right size may not fit your particular shape. There are no doubt as many variations of "life shape" as there are single moms, but they can grouped into some general categories.

DIVORCED

Many single moms have been married before. If you're one of them, you have both the benefits and the baggage of having once been part of an official twosome. Some of the benefits include the maturity (or the gray hairs) that can be gained only by having cohabited and coparented with another person. You know what it's like to commit, and you understand the peaks and valleys of relationships. However, the type of closeness that marriage fosters can have a dark side, too, namely, a loss of self or self-esteem, a feeling of being trapped, or simply being bored out of your mind.

Both how and why your marriage ended and the status of your current relationship with your ex are major factors in your ability to make wiser romantic choices this time around. You need to ask yourself how much of what you're looking for today is simply a reaction to what you've had in the past or if you're truly attuned to your own needs—and how those needs have evolved since you sashayed down the aisle and whispered "I do."

So to you millions of divorced single moms out there, I recommend taking some time to meditate on your marriage before you start looking for the next Mr. Right. I know that your marriage, even if it was a good one, is probably the last thing you want to think about right now. But just like when you're trying on a bikini in the harsh light of the dressing room, you're going to have to look in the mirror eventually so you might as well get it over with.

GET EX-RATED

You tell yourself you're over him. You tell everyone around you the same thing. But are you? Even if you don't spend much time thinking about your ex, are you still carrying around baggage from that relationship? Let's find out. Take this short quiz and get your very own ex-rating.

	YES	NO
1. If your ex asked you to come back today, would you consider it?	○	○
2. Do you find yourself comparing potential dates with your ex?	○	○
3. If you see your ex with another woman, do you get jealous?	○	○
4. Do you talk about your ex and your breakup more often than just every once in a while?	○	○
5. Have you recently cried out your ex's name during sex—even if you were only having sex with yourself?	○	○
6. Do you purposely talk about men you'd like to date in front of your ex? Or, if you're not dating, have you pictured yourself flaunting a new beau in front of him?	○	○

	YES	NO

7. Can you listen to songs, look at pictures, or watch movies that were once special to you and your ex without reaching for a box of tissues?   ○   ○

8. Are there still pictures of your ex or mementos from your relationship on prominent display around your house?   ○   ○

9. If your child talks about your ex, do you instantly feel anger or sadness?   ○   ○

10. If you were given the opportunity to harm your ex without getting caught, would you consider doing so?   ○   ○

Total up the number of "yes" answers to get your ex-rating:

0–2: Ex-cellent work! You've pretty much purged your past and are relationship-ready.

2–4: Ex-ercise your dating muscles. You've still got some baggage, but it's only the size of a small carry-on. Continue to unpack it while you explore new types of men.

4–6: Ex-cuse yourself from the dating scene until you've had more time to heal.

6 or more: Ex-pert help is needed. Find a good therapist (or exorcist) to help you get your ex out of your system for good.

WIDOWED

The loss of a partner is difficult enough, but once you start looking around for someone new you may find yourself feeling very guilty as well. As Coco Chanel once said, "Guilt is perhaps the most painful companion of death." Guilt is not good. Men in particular hate guilt. They can smell it. This is because they hate to be made to feel guilty about anything, and if you are feeling guilty about dating them, then somehow this will make them feel guilty and before you know it, they're gone. Got all that?

There are variations on this theme, of course. If your partnership wasn't all that great in the first place, you may feel little or no guilt about starting to move on. Or perhaps you helped him through a long illness, in which case you may be so exhausted that the only thing you should be shopping for right now is a nice spa vacation package.

Guilty or not guilty, you need to realize that in at least one way you're not that different from a single mom who is emerging from divorce and wants to start dating again: you are in a unique position to evaluate your past relationship and determine what worked for you and what didn't. This can be hard to do given the circumstances, and you must fight the tendency to put a halo on the head of your departed loved one, but it can also be very cathartic and can help with the healing and grieving process. Taking a long, hard look at what you had before, and what you might want to do differently this time around (or what worked for you particularly well and you are determined to find again), is an important step to take before you enter the dating scene.

SEPARATED

Plenty of people will tell you that separated women shouldn't date at all until they're divorced, but I'm not one of them. While I don't recommend you start searching for your *perfect* match while you're separated (because you won't have a clue what that might be), I do think it'll do you a lot of good to get out once in a while and be around positive, fun people. Separating is a painful and enormously draining process, especially when you have kids. You need to give yourself a break now and then, and it can be helpful to see that there are other men out there besides the one you've been sharing a bathroom with. However, you should make it clear to any guy you meet that you are not—I repeat, *not*—relationship or even fling material. You are only separated, which means that you are still married, and out of respect for yourself and your husband, you should try really hard to keep your clothes on and your heart off-limits.

UNMARRIED OR NEVER MARRIED

We've been called single mothers by choice or chance, as the case may be. What we are not called nearly often enough is legitimate. The stigma that comes with having a child on your own—whether you made a withdrawal at the sperm bank or simply forgot to pop in your diaphragm one lustful night—is a big ol' monkey on your back that you need to toss off before you reenter the dating scene. Even if you are blessedly ignorant of what others may think of you, you may meet a guy straight out of the gate who is very aware of it, or who isn't sure how he feels about your situation himself. Spending time with someone like that can wreak havoc on your self-esteem and perhaps even tempt you to take yourself off the market. Don't let that happen. Resolve any issues you have about being a single mom before you head out. Are you at peace with the choices you made back then? If the pregnancy was accidental and the father took off like a bat out of hell, do you feel abandoned and angry? Or was his exit actually a blessing in disguise and you feel lucky to have your child? It's critical that you have a strong emotional center, as well as friends and family who understand and support your decision to raise a child alone. Only then will you be ready to look carefully for guys who are enlightened.

Here's a tip: there seems to be a correlation between a guy's attitude toward single mothers and whether or not he had a stay-at-home mom. Guys with mothers who worked outside the home and those who were raised by single moms seem to get it more readily than those who are stuck in a time warp where dad brought home the bacon and mom cooked it, then did the dishes and still had time to make her little boy feel like the center of the universe. Those days are pretty much over, but guess what? Those guys are still around, and they might not be too keen on your choice to be a single mother. There are always exceptions, and I'm sure there are lots of men who were raised in a traditional two-parent home with a stay-at-home mom who will be perfectly accepting of you. If you know where these guys are hiding, though, drop me a line, will ya?

> "Most people don't understand what your life is like, and what they imagine it to be is based on TV movies and cultural stereotypes, which are wrong almost all the time. Try to forgive their ignorance—but also try to find someone who is not ignorant!"
>
> —Carrie, 37, Boston

Got Style?

Now you know your size and your shape. You're out there, shopping like a madwoman for love and sex. So what do you do once you come across something you'd like to try on? Make sure it's your style, of course.

For example, I never wear polka dots. I don't know why, but I just don't. I'm not comfortable in them. I shy away from stripes for the most part, too. Likewise, men who are too busy or loud (those who like to call attention to themselves) really turn me off.

The point is that, just like your taste in fashion, you likely have some specific tastes in men. Here again, however, you might take a bit of time to consider if your style has changed somewhat since you became a single mom—or, if it hasn't, whether it should. When you finally find someone you really like, ask yourself the following questions to determine whether he truly fits your style.

CAN YOU AFFORD IT?

Nothing is more irritating than finding a smashing outfit that fits great and makes you look really hot—and costs so much you nearly burst into tears.

The same thing can happen when you're in the market for a man. You may get really lucky and find someone who fits you like a glove. Then you realize that you simply can't afford him right now. You don't have the time or the energy required to nurture the relationship. You're tired all the time, you're working your tush off, and your six-year-old is having problems at school. You are, to put it mildly, not in the right space for a relationship.

And so you have to give this perfect fit a pass. You'll be bummed for a while. Just tell yourself that if you're meant to have him, he'll be around next season, and by then you may be better equipped to fit him into your life.

A TRULY GREAT FIND

I was upset. My twins were three months old and my boyfriend was acting like a jerk. I wasn't sleeping, I felt totally alone, and I didn't know what to do. So naturally I went shopping.

Not looking for anything in particular, I stumbled into a charming little interior design store. That's where I met a mother-and-daughter design team, wonderful women who befriended me in my sad-sack state and helped me through some very rough days. That day the store was quiet and, sensing my distress, the lovely ladies invited me to sit down on one of their very expensive chintz chairs. I sobbed out my story. My guy was becoming more distant since the boys had been born; he was self-absorbed and literally driving me crazy. The daughter, a beautiful single mom in her early forties, put her hands on my shoulders and looked me square in the eye. She said, "You don't understand. Everything's different now." I panicked. What did she mean? Couldn't things stay just as they were, even though I had two screaming infants attached to me 24-7 and my heart was breaking? Did she mean things would get harder? They were already hard enough!

She noticed my deer-in-the-headlights look and gently took my hand. "You don't understand this yet, but you will.

Once you have a child, what you're looking for totally changes. If someone isn't right, you give him the boot right away. It's a blessing, really. It stops us from wasting time on guys that aren't worth it, like we used to before we were moms." She said this calmly and with complete confidence, with the wisdom that can come only from having been there.

It did take me a while to understand what she meant, and, like many single moms, I fought this new way of doing things for some time. I was still the "old me" who liked narcissistic artists and charming poor guys and extremely good-looking guys and, most of all, guys who weren't able to commit. I had to beat myself up a bit more, grow into being a mom, and grow closer to my sons before I finally figured out what this lovely woman meant that day.

You may have to do the same. You likely won't get it right out of the box, and that's okay. So if you're confused and scared and not sure what you want, give yourself a breather. Get out of the house. Go shopping. You may pick up something really special—like good advice and a shoulder to lean on. Now that's priceless.

DO YOU HAVE ONE JUST LIKE IT IN YOUR CLOSET ALREADY?

Why do I have thirty pairs of black shoes? Because every time I go shopping I see some black shoes that I like, even though I probably have two pairs exactly like them gathering dust at home. The same thing can happen when you're looking for a partner. By choosing the same type again and again you don't have to leave your comfort zone—even if that zone is crammed with men who make you miserable.

Force yourself to expand your horizons—and your taste in men. I'm not suggesting you start to date starving artists if you're typically drawn to Wall Street wizards, but just like when you choose to wear bright orange instead of basic black, exploring the range of options available to you can give you a much-needed jolt in the romance department.

DOES IT HAVE TO BE DRY-CLEANED?

Impracticality is the stuff fashion fortunes are made of. Designers are in the business of creating new trends each year so that they can continue to go to St. Barts in the winter and rehab every summer. And guess what? We are only too happy to pay their way. We follow their lead and adopt whatever style is making headlines, no matter how ridiculous or expensive.

Likewise, some men are simply more high maintenance than others. These self-absorbed guys are demanding, they like to be noticed, and they are never on time. But when you're with them, you feel *so* alive, so charged up. They are also experts at keeping you guessing.

If your style leans toward wash-and-wear—in other words, you prefer things that are comfortable and long-lasting—then leave the flashy goods alone. After all, as a single mom, your life is high-maintenance enough already.

WHAT WILL YOUR CHILDREN
THINK OF YOU IN IT?

When my boys were just four years old, I remember parading out of my bedroom in a new dress I hoped to wear on a date that night. Not expecting them to pay much attention to me, much less answer me, I asked, "How do I look?" They stared at me for what seemed like a long time. Finally, one of my sons said very seriously, "That dress is *ugly.*" I stood there and waited for him to start laughing, assuming he was teasing. He wasn't. He was totally serious. When I took another look in the full-length mirror, I realized he was dead-on: the dress was ugly. Butt ugly.

After that, I often asked my kids how I looked in something, always keeping in mind that they only recently learned to dress themselves. Still, their opinions are often uncannily accurate—and this includes their take on people. I have been very careful to limit their exposure to my romantic partners, and in fact I have introduced them to only two boyfriends, both of whom I was seriously involved with. Their sixth sense proved to be flawless; they often expressed doubts about my former boyfriend, who turned out to be a complete ass.

So before you date someone, ask yourself, if your kids were ever to meet him, would they give him a thumbs-up or thumbs-down?

> *"Children are a great litmus test. The presence of children tends to weed out men who are simply looking to hook up."*
> —Stephanie, 32, *New Hampshire*

WHAT IS THE RETURN POLICY?

I am unbelievably lazy when it comes to returning purchases. I put it off, telling myself I'll wear it someday, then end up giving it to Goodwill and wasting precious money on a ridiculous fashion faux pas. Do we do the same thing with men? You betcha. Breaking up with someone just seems to be harder for women than it is for men. I realize this is a generalization, but in my experience and that of many of my friends, it's completely true. That's why it's so important to determine early on how easy or difficult it may be to end a romance with someone. I know it seems counterintuitive to try and get a feel for what it might be like to dump a guy before you've even gotten involved with him, but it can save you a lot of grief in the long run. Women who have been abused or threatened, in particular, are wise to have their antennae up for men who might be overly possessive or jealous. These guys are like crazy glue, sticking to you so desperately that you end up ripping yourself apart trying to break free. So save yourself the prospect of a bad ending from the very beginning by steering clear of the too-intense types and going for the Velcro guys instead. After all, it's okay to make a little noise when you separate, as long as both of you can eventually part ways unscathed.

ARE YOU BUYING THIS JUST TO
MAKE YOURSELF FEEL BETTER?

What's the difference between a shopaholic and a sex or love addict? Not much, really. Both expend their resources irresponsibly in order to achieve a short-term boost in their self-esteem. Is your romantic style a little too intense? Do you tend to go for guys who feed your ego, then leave you feeling like you've had the wind knocked out of you? If so, look for love very, very carefully. Try hard to resist those that you know, deep inside, will leave your heart as empty as a shopaholic's wallet.

"I think that before someone actively looks for a partner she needs to feel good about herself as an individual and as a mom. So many women look for someone because they cannot be alone. That's not the answer. You need to feel good about yourself before you can put energy into a relationship."

—*Kelly, 37, Maine*

Forget Buyer Beware— It's Buyer Aware

All of this stuff about size, shape, and style may have you feeling a little overwhelmed. After all, your life is full of lists, demands, and things to think about. You may be asking yourself why your love life has to be hard work, too. But knowing what you want and knowing what works best for you can only make your life easier in the long run. Think of it as working a little harder to save up for something you really want so you can buy it free and clear. You may have to forgo immediate gratification, but your patience will be rewarded.

Still, don't be afraid to rewrite, edit, or even toss out your romantic shopping list altogether and start fresh. Be flexible with yourself and with others while striving to maintain a core set of beliefs about who you are and what you want in a partner. As Dr.

Pepper Schwartz puts it, "We don't want to be too regimented. You're free to make bold or new choices—take advantage of that. It's a delicate balance of being open and spontaneous and knowing when to pull up the drawbridge if something doesn't seem to be the right fit for you. And of entering the entire process informed and aware."

Now that you've made your shopping list for love, it's time to take stock of your looks (and your attitude). You'll even get to do some *actual* shopping this time.

chapter three

The

Single Mom

Makeover

HOW TO GET A GREAT GUY
TO ASK YOU OUT—OR, AT THE
VERY LEAST, CHECK YOU OUT

"There is no cosmetic for beauty like happiness."
—Maria Mitchell (1818–89),
the first professional female astronomer in the United States

*"Sex appeal is fifty percent what you've got and
fifty percent what people think you've got."*
—Sophia Loren

———————————————

*T*here is an army of single mothers out there, and like any good army, we have our very own uniform. It is comprised of sweats, T-shirts, tennis shoes, ponytails, and a perpetually exhausted look. This kind of outfit may reflect our lives spent in the trenches of single parenthood—but it isn't going to turn any guy's head.

And even when we manage to spruce up our exterior, often our insides are not all that pretty. As single moms, we must constantly deal with a number of stresses and ego-battering circumstances that many childless or married women do not. Whether we're doing battle with our boss, our ex, our bank account, or our teenager, we are fighting fires on many fronts. These seemingly relentless challenges can leave us feeling defeated at times, and ultimately they can damage the way we look, too. The bad news is that many of these stresses aren't going to disappear anytime soon. The good news is that by beautifying your inner being you will be better equipped to handle what the world has to dish out, and at the same time you will achieve an outer glow that will be hard to resist.

Beauty and the Beast

You know the drill. In your desire to attract a potential mate, you go *way* out of your way to look beautiful. You wax, polish, pluck, and primp. You sprinkle sparkly dust on your décolletage, curl your eyelashes into 90-degree angles, and slather on mascara. You paint your lips like Picasso, expertly layering on liner, lipstick, and gloss.

You look in the mirror. You look good, stunning even.

So how come you *feel* so damn ugly?

Girls, let's face it. Mom was right. Beauty begins on the *inside*. So before we talk about physical beauty, let's work on making over your mind.

For starters, I'm going to ask that you take a good, long look at yourself in the mirror. Then complete the following exercise.

- Make a list of all the ugly thoughts you have about yourself. Write down everything from "I hate the way my thighs rub together when I walk" to "I get angry too quickly."

- In a column next to that list, make a list of all the ugly thoughts you have about men: either men in general or particular men who may have hurt you in the past.

- Now think of someone who is outwardly beautiful, who has all the right features, but somehow still seems unattractive to you. There's just something about them that would make you reluctant to spend any time with them (Paris Hilton fits the bill for me). Cut out a picture of this person and tape it to your bathroom mirror along with your list of ugly thoughts.

- Now make a list of all the things you love about yourself. No object of affection is too small, from the constellation of tiny freckles on your arm to the elegant shape of your feet, to the way you stop for people in crosswalks no matter how much of a hurry you're in. Get it all down on paper.

- Next to this column, make a list of all the beautiful things that come to mind when you think of men, again, either men in general or men you've known.

- Now think of someone you know, or know of, who epitomizes inner and outer beauty (I personally think of Oprah Winfrey and the actress Cate Blanchett). It could be a coworker, a friend, or a relative who simply radiates beauty and confidence from the inside out. Paste that person's picture, along with your beauty list, next to the first picture you displayed. Even better, imprint this person's image in your psyche.

- Every time you look in the mirror and see this little collage staring back at you, take ten seconds to ask yourself which list you want to keep adding to and which one you want to trash. Ponder for a minute which person you'd like to emulate and which one you never, *ever* want to be compared to.

- One by one, face and then eliminate your ugly thoughts. This is easier to do if you simultaneously add items to the list of beautiful thoughts you have about yourself. At some point that mole on the back of your neck will seem pretty insignificant in light of the fact that you have gorgeous eyes and also happen to be a great kisser.

This process may seem a bit silly at first, and you may be embarrassed to have these lists and pictures out in the open for all to see, but defining what beauty means to you and listing which parts of yourself you feel are unattractive and need making over can be really empowering. It's like when you finally have the guts to cut your hair after you've been painstakingly growing it out for eighteen months. Sure, it's long, but it's also a pain in the ass, it weighs you down, and it makes you look a lot older. When you whack it off, you feel free, unburdened, and more open to the world around you. The same thing will happen when you confront and destroy the beasts within you and reveal your innate beauty.

Get Glowing

Remember when you were pregnant—those rare moments in between vomiting, constipation, breakouts, exhaustion and massive weight gain—when you positively glowed from the inside out? You were beautiful as never before. Why? Because by carrying a child within you, you felt good about yourself and what you were doing. You loved yourself and the miracle that was taking place inside your body. And people noticed—men in particular— even if you didn't notice them noticing you. Now, I'm not suggesting you go get knocked up so you can look hot. I'm trying to get you to remember what inner beauty *feels* like. Your mission is to do what's necessary to recapture that feeling every day. Here are just a few of the ways you can light yourself up from the inside:

- Volunteer

- Exercise

- Create: draw, paint, write, design, or sculpt

- Pray or meditate

- Garden

- Play with your kids

- Experience nature

- Play music, sing, or dance

- Do something nice for a friend

- Do something nice for yourself

Beauty and health expert Kat James knows a thing or two about makeovers, having completely made herself over while building a phenomenal career as a beauty consultant to celebrities such as Sarah Jessica Parker, Kate Hudson, and others. The author of the book *The Truth about Beauty* and the host of the PBS show of the same name told me that "being beautiful on the inside is not only being a good person; it's being accountable to yourself by being an advocate for yourself and acting on empowering information. This actually builds self-esteem as powerfully or more powerfully than just practicing a 'feel-good philosophy.'"

Outward Bound

Once you're satisfied that you look and feel flawless on the inside, you can get started on the really fun part: transforming your exterior. Like any remodeling project, there are various degrees of renovation you can attempt, and only you can decide how much time, money, and energy you want to spend on redoing yourself. But since you're a single mom, I'd recommend starting with ways to make yourself over that are cheap, easy, and childproof.

CLOTHES CALL

When you became a mom, did you suddenly decide that it somehow wouldn't be appropriate to wear youngish, hip, or slightly revealing clothes? Whether you wanted to hide post-baby weight gain or prevent the prissy women at your Mommy and Me group from giving you snotty looks, you may have felt you had to suppress the fun side of your fashion sense for a while. Not surprisingly, I think this is ridiculous. Is there anything sexier or more attractive than a mother who has obviously taken the time to keep up with trends and pull together a cool look? I think not. Even if a few extra pounds are stubbornly refusing to head for the exits, that doesn't mean your closet must be filled only with baggy sweat suits, or—even worse—your old maternity clothes. That oversized denim shirt you lived in when seven months pregnant is fine to wear while painting the bedroom but, like a grounded teenager, *it absolutely must not leave the house.*

So now what? If you toss out all of your old favorites, will you be standing there butt naked? Good. This gives you an opportunity to start fresh. "But I'm broke," you say. I know, because I say that a lot. Well, remember all the hard work you put in on beautifying your interior? Here's where it pays off: you need to be creative, confident, and open-minded in order to build a great wardrobe on the cheap.

Here are some of my shopping secrets, gleaned during some mighty lean years of living on the financial margins.

Yard Sales

My best friend turned me on to yard sales twenty years ago, but it took me a while to feel comfortable buying used clothes from total strangers. I was delighted to find an antique end table for ten bucks or a new set of dishes for five, but a linen suit that someone else wore to work? Nah. Then I suddenly became poor and all my pride went out the window. Now I'm absolutely addicted. You never know when you'll come across a yard sale organized by a woman with a great eye for cool clothes. Even better, at these sales you'll often discover pieces that have been barely, or even never, worn at all. It's also a great way to meet interesting like-minded women—they often like to tell you where they bought that designer jacket and how much they loved it, but they never wore it so, hey, you can have it for a buck. So don't be shy, scope out the neighborhood sales, and you could end up with a whole slew of new stuff for under twenty clams.

Thrift Shops

Though they aren't quite as inexpensive as yard sales, thrift shops are still a source for incredible bargains, and the great thing about shopping at them is that the clothes are generally well organized and clearly priced, which saves you time and energy. You'll also be glad to know that lots of people bring their kids to thrift stores, so you don't need to feel guilty if yours run up and down the aisles playing hide-and-seek in the racks while you browse.

Pregnant Friends

Remember when your tummy first started to swell? You were probably absolutely thrilled and immediately ran out to buy clothes in bigger sizes. Pregnancy is the only time in our lives when we are happy to go up a size or two. Or three. If you have a friend who is shopping for a maternity wardrobe, she likely needs to make some room in her closet. Offer to help her out by taking some of those outfits you've envied all these years off her hands.

Outlet Stores

Even factoring in the insane price of gas, it can be worth the long drive into the middle of nowhere to visit an outlet mall, especially if you have a job that requires you look good five days a week. You might even have an uppity personal assistant who is sure to comment if you wear the same suit more than twice in a month. A word of caution, however: though the prices are discounted, these designer duds were probably overpriced to begin with, so try not to go nuts at the outlet mall. Bring only one credit card, ideally one with a low limit, because if you overspend and decide you want to take some stuff back, it's a long drive back to the boonies.

Single Mom Clothes Exchange

If you're part of a single mom's support group, consider organizing a swap meet every couple of months, where you and your friends can trade stuff you no longer wear. It's fun and, best of all, it's totally *free*—a four letter word I'm quite fond of.

> "We may not have the thin bodies or stretch-mark-free bodies of other women, but we are still beautiful. Understand that 'post-natal' doesn't carry on into the toddler years. At some point you'll have to realize there is a sexy, confident body hiding under those sweats. So get to the mall and buy that skirt."
>
> —Julie, 21, Boston

> "I shop at consignment shops for designer labels and fun new items. They are available at a fraction of the original cost and must be presented clean and in like-new condition. I also go to department stores to peruse their makeup counters and sample the products, then look for knockoffs at drug stores. The quality does suffer a bit, but if you don't have the budget for quality makeup, the other stuff will do. Most men don't like a lot of fuss anyway and prefer you go natural, with your hair down and minimal makeup."
>
> —Lee, 29, Seattle

WILL ANY BODY DO?

Finding new clothes is one thing; fitting into them is an altogether different challenge. Even if you're comfortable with how much you weigh, how do you feel about how those pounds are distributed? What about physical endurance, which is so critical for our high-stress lives? Are you spending more time in line at Starbucks waiting to get pumped up on caffeine (I have to admit, I practically live there) than you are pumping iron?

    If there is one complaint I hear constantly from single moms, it's that they don't have the time or energy to exercise. Here's what I'd like to know: Since I'm always running after my kids, picking up toys, lifting the laundry basket, carrying groceries, climbing stairs, and throwing the ball for my boys, why am I not as buff as those chicks on the cover of *Shape* magazine? Is there *no* reward for my daily exertions?

Well, other than a clean house, not really. Sure, these activities burn a few calories, but the truth is that you need a sustained exercise regimen in order to get the body you want. Here again, we are confronted with the dual challenges of time and cost. Not to worry, though: with a little creativity you can overcome these obstacles and be on your way to building a body that will drive the guys crazy.

> *"Kids love to be outside, so take them for long walks or on bike rides and you'll get exercise while they do. Kids also need lots of fruit and veggies. If you eat them too, it sets a good example."*
>
> —*Carrie, 37, Boston*

FIT TO BE TIED (UP, PERHAPS?)

Joining a gym is great, but it's not the only solution for getting your body moving. Besides, gyms can be expensive, and even those with child care limit the amount of time you can leave your children and often charge an additional fee. Gyms can be a good place to meet guys, so I'm not saying you shouldn't join one. But you might want to consider these cheap and easy alternatives as well:

- Play with your kids. You should be doing this anyway, but if your involvement is typically limited to kicking the soccer ball once and heading back into the house, you're not taking advantage of what can be both a great workout and an opportunity to spend time with your children. So instead of just booting the ball a couple of times, play a full game. Or set up drills and don't just stand on the sidelines—do them yourself. If your kids are small and not yet able to play sports, get out the stroller and they can ride while you walk. Go up a few hills; jog if you can. You'll be sweating in no time, and your wee one will likely fall asleep on the way back from the park.

- Join a biking, hiking, or walking club. You can probably find many women in your area who are looking for others to exercise with. Check out www.craigslist.org to start, or post a flyer at your workplace or local daycare. This is a great way to socialize while you sweat.

- Get a workout buddy. If you want fast results and help with motivation, consider splitting the cost of a personal trainer with a friend.

- Set up a home gym. This doesn't have to cost much, and it may be the only way you'll ever really get to exercise. Get some good workout or yoga tapes, a portable stair-climber (you can find used ones pretty cheap), and some free weights. Paste a sign on the door that instructs your children to stay out while you exercise or you'll make them do thirty push-ups.

ORAL FIXATIONS

If you manage to establish a consistent exercise program, good for you! But if you're still shoveling down the junk food, knock it off— it's bad for you. I know this is really difficult with kids in the house. The door to the snack cabinet is always open, and the kids seem to always be in it. And because you never have time to prepare healthy meals for yourself, chances are you're digging in there as well.

But if you want to change your diet and exercise habits for good, take a slow, steady, and well-informed approach to weight control.

"Forget cold turkey and the drill-sergeant approach to self-improvement," Kat James says. "Life is harsh enough, and besides, the approach you see on extreme makeover shows does not transform us for real."

MAKEOVER—OR UNDER?

Some years back, I pretty much stopped wearing makeup. I still use a smidge of blush and a little lipstick, but that's about it, unless it's a very special occasion in the evening, in which case I'll really go to town and lay on a little mascara and eye shadow.

"I know this sounds shallow, but look good all the time! You just never know when or where you're going to run into someone. Don't get into the sweat suit/hair in a ponytail rut. I've been there, and it's really hard to get out. Add a kid to that look and no one will notice you. Make time to exercise—you'll be healthier and feel better about yourself. Plus, if the clothes are coming off with a new person, you'll feel a lot better if you've been going to the gym."

—Alison, 39, San Francisco

I pared down my use of cosmetics long before I became a single mom—and I immediately noticed I looked younger and my skin had far fewer breakouts. Now that I'm a mom, I can't imagine having a high-maintenance makeup routine. Neither should you. When you think about how you can quickly and easily improve your looks, steer clear of the cosmetics counter, where those robotlike ladies in the white lab coats are just waiting to "transform" you using a slew of overpriced products. Instead, get naked. Start with your skin as bare and exposed as a baby's bottom at bath time, stand in front of the mirror, and look closely at your face. You may be so accustomed to hiding under a variety of cosmetics that you don't recognize the person staring back at you.

"Start from a clean slate and focus on a healthy, self-centered, deconstructed approach to beauty," advises beauty guru Kat James. In her book *The Truth about Beauty*, she advises that you use less makeup, or even go without it, on weekends if not on weekdays. "Find as many things as you can to like about your naked face," she says. "As you begin to grow comfortable with it, others will, too."

The minimalist approach to makeup is particularly suited for single moms, who are short on time and often sleep-deprived. Plastering on foundation, powder, and blush over tired skin really just makes you look more fatigued—and a lot older. Instead, use a good face mask to wake up your sleepy skin. Rather than blowing your budget on pricey lipsticks and eyeliner, splurge on high-quality skin care products—lotions, exfoliants, eye creams—that will help preserve and protect your precious skin. And don't forget that the best way to obtain a healthy, rosy glow on your cheeks is by exercising.

CREATE A "BEAUTY JAR"

I don't know about you, but I *never* have the oil in my car changed every three thousand miles, and for the longest time I didn't maintain my hair and skin with any regularity, either. This meant that at some point, like my poor neglected car, I would break down—I wouldn't be fit to go anywhere—especially on a date. Of course, beauty maintenance costs money, something many single moms are often without.

So one day, when I was looking particularly like a hag, I took a picture of myself and taped it to a jar. Then I fished around in the bottom of my purse, scrounged in the backseat of my probably-needs-an-oil-change car, and finally opened up my wallet. I put all the money I'd scraped together into the jar (a whopping $12) and *voila*, the beauty jar was born. This is how you can make one for yourself.

1. Tape a particularly horrible picture of yourself—you know, the one where your roots are showing and your skin looks like the surface of the moon—to a jar. In this picture you must look tired, stressed, and very, very ugly.

2. Every week, put $20—cash, no checks—into the jar. And no raiding the kids' piggy banks—you must do this for yourself. At the end of six weeks, you should have $120 or so. Go get your hair cut and colored and a half-hour facial. Depending on where you live, you may need to sweeten the pot with another twenty or thirty bucks.

3. When you get home, feeling beautiful and refreshed, start the process over again. Never, *ever* stop doing this. Not only is this

experience a wonderful treat for yourself, it's what's called basic maintenance, the kind that's necessary if you hope to appeal to the opposite sex.

By the way, I still never remember to change the oil in my car. But at least if my car breaks down and I have to hitchhike or take the bus, I'll be looking damn good while I do it.

FANTASTIC PLASTIC

Except for the likes of Cher and Pamela Anderson, I don't personally have a problem with cosmetic procedures such as botox or collagen. And if you want to go up a breast size or deny gravity for a few more years, breast augmentation or a breast lift is an option as well. But we single moms have to consider more than how much it's gonna hurt, such as the cost and the recovery time, for starters. If you don't have an extra thirty minutes to exercise every day, do you really have a couple of weeks to spend in bed nursing your tender ta tas? And what do you say to your children? Aren't we always telling them they don't need to look like the people they see on TV? You're a bit of a hypocrite if you find yourself envying some starlet's perfect C cups and then run out to get a pair just like hers.

As part of your overall makeover process, it's okay to consult with a plastic surgeon if you think some minor alteration might give you the added boost you need to get out there with complete confidence. However, if you're expecting any procedure to make up for a lack of self-esteem or to fix other problems with your love life, don't waste your time or money. After all, a whole truckload of operations hasn't made Michael Jackson any happier.

A growing trend is for women to alter their looks below the waist. They do this either by waxing, which hurts like hell but is noninvasive, or by having a labiaplasty. In her book, *Vaginas: An Owner's Manual*, Dr. Carol Livoti takes on both of these cosmetic procedures with aplomb. "My days of pelvic exams reveal that there is less and less hair on the labia majora as the years have gone by. The Mohican look, as I call it, is just a strip of hair at the top of the mons—a token remnant. The very popular Brazilian wax denudes almost the entire exterior genitalia of hair. I don't know that there are any health hazards associated with removing your pubic hair, but it sure must hurt. And there are many unfortunate women who, in their dogged pursuit of fashion, have made their genitalia more unsightly with ingrown hairs, pimples and rashes— a common result of waxing."

For us moms, a more important issue may be that things are perhaps a little too loose down there, thanks to the experience of childbirth. Many women who want a tighter fit during intercourse are now considering vaginoplasty, a pricey surgical procedure that is not without its risks. We'll talk more about this procedure, along with far less radical ways to rejuvenate your genitalia, in Chapter Seven.

In the Eye of the Beholder

Let's be honest. If we believed that men were attracted to us for our hearts and minds first and our looks second, would we even bother with all of this stuff? Sure, we'd still want to take care of our health and exercise and brush our teeth every day, but the truth is that making yourself look great is a necessary part of the mating ritual. Most men I know would readily admit they are shallower than their female counterparts and that they initially notice the way a woman looks and only then pay attention to her personality. By making ourselves feel and look as great as we can, we increase our odds of getting a guy's attention.

That's fine, but we also need to remember that looking hot is no guarantee you'll have a sizzling love life. There are plenty of stunning female celebrities who whine endlessly about how no one ever asks them out. So even if you transform yourself head to toe and don't land a hot date right away, don't despair.

"You have to remember you've experienced rejection before. Interaction with others is risky. That's the deal—that's the lifelong deal," says Dr. Pepper Schwartz. "And remember not to take it personally. You have to believe in yourself, and then take yourself on this adventure."

Now you know what you want, and you feel good about the way you look. All you need is to find a great guy to go out with. Let the adventure begin.

chapter four

The Good, the Bad, and the Truly Ugly

X-RAY VISION, SUPERSONIC HEARING, AND A BUILT-IN LIE DETECTOR: TOOLS TO HELP YOU FIND A DECENT GUY

"Trust yourself. You know more than you think you do."
—Dr. Benjamin Spock

"Women cannot complain about men anymore
until they start getting better taste in them."
—Bill Maher

If I knew the secret to finding the perfect man, I would be wealthy beyond words. What I do know is that by not wasting time on the *wrong* guys, you can conserve your precious energy for a man who truly deserves you. It is this crucial step of pre-screening potential suitors that many single moms overlook in their pursuit of romantic happiness.

I have many ideas (and some strong opinions) about where to meet interesting eligible men. But before we go there, you need to learn how to discover which guys are good, which ones are bad, and which ones are truly ugly.

Burn That Flag

You're no doubt familiar with the notion of "red flags" that should warn you away from certain new men. Single moms, however, need to go above and beyond the typical tired advice that we've been hearing for years. For example, if he shows up two hours late for your first date, this could be a warning sign. (No kidding). Instead, forget about looking for red flags—that metaphor is *way* too wimpy.

Think instead of a twenty-foot-tall, bright-red flashing neon sign with a siren on top. Your bad-guy warning system must be impossible to ignore, because if you disregard the danger signals that inevitably appear when you date many guys, it'll end up costing you much more emotionally than it would a woman without children. Sure, a childless single woman will pay for neglecting the warning signs, too, but as a single mom you can't just sit around and lick your wounds or dash out with your girlfriends to get sauced on apple martinis when you get dumped. No, you have school lunches to make, soccer games to attend, an ex to deal with, and a lawn to mow. Toss a bad romantic experience into that stressful mix and all of a sudden you're really on the edge, or you've gone over it altogether.

So let's avoid a bad end by getting it right from the start. I recommend you use my own personal technique for separating the wheat from the chaff. It's called the Single Mom As Superhero (S.M.A.S.H.) method, and it is guaranteed to help you destroy your romantic bad habits once and for all.

As we all know from watching an endless array of summer release movies with our children, all superheroes have superpowers. You do too, yet like many of the characters in these films, you may not even know you have them. Your secret weapons for successful dating are within you; you just need to learn how to use them.

Superpower #1: X-Ray Vision

I know what you're thinking. If you had X-ray vision, you could see what a guy has going on below the belt right away. That would be nice, but you're better off aiming a little higher at first, where his heart resides.

After a particularly bad run of men, when I was bemoaning the fact that I just never saw it coming, a much wiser girlfriend said something that stuck with me all these years. "Trust me, if you're paying attention, a guy will show his true self pretty quickly. They're not very good at hiding it."

The critical piece of her invaluable advice is that we should *pay attention*. Take your eyes off of his nice pecs or cool designer shoes long enough to notice the little things. God is in the details, as they say, and so is the devil. Here are some examples of what you should be looking for.

LOOK INTO HIS EYES

I'm not suggesting you have a staring contest, but the old cliché that the eyes are the window to the soul is really on to something. Recent research involving thermal imaging even suggests that when people are lying, they get "hot spots" around their eyes because the amount of blood that circulates to the capillaries under the skin around the eyes increases. Obviously, you can't carry your own miniature thermal imaging device around in your purse (although I think someone should invent one!), so try to make frequent eye contact with him and see how it feels. Does he look away quickly? Are his eyes more focused on the sexy waitress that keeps strolling past than they are on you? Are they bloodshot? Even worse, is he wearing those awful contact lenses that alter his eye color and make him look like he's from outer space? Truly, when it comes to sizing up a guy quickly, the eyes have it.

TAKE A GOOD LOOK AT HIS HANDS

Try *not* to focus on their size and what this may or may not mean about the size of his manhood. Instead, notice whether they are clean and well cared for. Even if he works in an industry where they are subject to a good amount of wear and tear, has he taken the time to keep them manicured? If he goes out of the house with dirty mitts, can you even imagine what his home must look like? Unless dirt really turns you on, you may want to skip holding hands with this dude. After all, we have enough grime and germs around our house with kids at home, and who needs more? And always, *always* check his left hand for a pale band of flesh where his wedding ring would normally be. Unless he's already disclosed a recent separation or divorce, there's only one thing that can mean. Finally, pay attention to where his hands are most of the time. Are his paws all over you? Do they have a death grip on a beer glass that he just can't seem to let go of? Hands down, taking a close look at this part of a guy's anatomy can reveal plenty.

LOOK VERY, VERY CLOSELY AT
HOW HE BEHAVES WITH HIS FRIENDS

When you're out for the evening, all you want to do is have fun, socialize, and relax for a change. You can do that later, after your guy has passed the S.M.A.S.H. smell test. For now, you need to scrutinize his behavior carefully. When guys think you're not looking, they let down their guard. This is when you switch on your X-ray vision. Does he join in when his friends start gawking at or coming on to the pretty young things that pass by? Or does he look a little embarrassed for his buddies? Does he concur when one of his friends starts trashing his ex-girlfriend, or does he remain politely silent? Obviously, you don't want to date a social moron. He should be able to join in a good time and easily interact with others—but without resorting to obnoxious, juvenile behavior.

OKAY, JUST FOR FUN, TRY TO IMAGINE HIM NAKED

This is where *real* X-ray vision would come in handy.

Superpower #2: Supersonic Hearing

More than once a guy has reminded me that he told me what a jerk he was when we first started dating—I just wasn't listening. Interestingly, they tend to say this in the middle of a breakup, thereby shifting blame for the split from their horrible behavior squarely onto my shoulders. This is a shitty thing to do, but not completely unjustified. Men will very often tell you of their failings very early in a relationship:

Guy: "I've been volunteering at the animal shelter ever since I got out of prison."

Gal: "Wow, you volunteer at the animal shelter? That is so cool."

Get my point? We don't listen to what we don't want to hear.

Sometimes, however, these revelations aren't so obvious; they might be couched in a way that is designed not to cause alarm or incite further questioning. A guy naturally tends to downplay his bad features and play up the good, but there is a fine line between putting his best foot forward and purposely deceiving you. In order to discern the difference, you need to start using your second superpower: supersonic hearing.

LISTEN UP!

When a guy uses any of these of hot-button words or phrases when talking about his life, your ears should prick up:

- Broke
- Angry
- Sex addiction
- Drunk
- Kids are a pain
- Affair

- Psycho bitch ex-wife
- Fired
- Depressed
- Commitment issues
- Anything racist
- My mom always says . . .

This list could go on and on. The point is that little things say a lot. If he's not careful enough to at least try to hide some of his failings, he could be testing you to see how much he can get away with. Or he could be trying in his own lame way to warn you about his shortcomings, so that later, when you call him a commitment-phobic, child-hating loser, he can say, "But I told you so." It's your mission, then, to discover the real story behind his words. Don't be afraid to ask him what he means when he says his ex-wife is a psycho bitch from hell, because she may indeed be one, in which case his rant is justified (though still mostly inappropriate). Otherwise, if you never open your mouth to understand what's coming out of his, you have no one to blame later but yourself.

HEARING AIDS

Did you know bats have sonar hearing so finely tuned that they can hear the footsteps of an insect? Let that be an inspiration to you. I know that a furry flying rat that sleeps upside down and carries rabies isn't exactly an appealing role model, but guess what? Bats are great survivors, and their hearing ability has a lot to do with their resiliency. If you're going to sort through the many unworthy men out there and find your dream date, you need to start using your supercharged hearing skills.

To do this, start by turning off your motor mouth. Instead, make an effort to really listen to a guy. Not only is this polite, it will inspire him to fill the chasm of silence between you. You can help him along by asking him seemingly innocuous questions about himself: Does he like his job? What kind of movies does he like? Does he have family nearby? These queries may seem bland, but they have the potential to open up a Pandora's box of information about him. When he starts talking about work, for instance, use your finely tuned hearing to pick up on his anxiety and anger, or is it excitement and enthusiasm? Discussing his family can reveal plenty about how a guy feels about relationships and having a family of his own, which gets you very close to the topic of how he feels about dating a single mom.

Later, when you're alone, think about the things he said. If any of it seems a little off, or worthy of further investigation, make a mental note of it. Is all of this scrutiny really necessary, you may ask? Hell, yes. Listening carefully puts you in control of the situation, allowing you to avoid being snowed and to make informed decisions about whom to date. Let's not forget that one of the things we most often complain about as mothers is that our children never listen to us. Isn't it time we acknowledged we're not exactly pros in that department either and do something about it? Come on, Batgirl—perk up your ears.

Superpower #3: A Built-in Lie Detector

Women are saddled with all kinds of challenges that men never have to face. From menstruation to pregnancy to menopause, it often seems like we get the raw end of the deal. However, there is one attribute we have that men will never possess: feminine intuition. Sure, some guys are intuitive. But when it comes to pure gut instinct, we definitely have the edge.

Your intuition is perhaps your greatest superpower and, unlike the two powers previously discussed, you don't have to do much to learn how to use it. You simply have to listen to your inner voice. Unfortunately, in our desire to date we often willfully ignore it. We don't want to believe it, and sometimes we even hate it— especially when it turns out to be right.

Yet your intuition is a gift, is it not? Hasn't it helped you as a mother? Not only can you always tell when your kid is lying, but often you can sense when your child is in jeopardy or upset or hungry or sick, even if he or she exhibits no outward signs.

The challenge is to keep your gut instinct separate from your romantic fantasies. An intense crush or powerful lust can drown out even the loudest inner voice. So when you are particularly smitten with someone, you need to go to Herculean lengths to ensure you're allowing your intuition to do its work. One way to do this is to set aside a good chunk of time when you vow not to think about him at all. Do anything else—go to the movies, fold laundry, clean the toilet. And in those most mundane of moments, your intuition will let you know if this is a guy to be excited about—or if trouble lies ahead. You may not be able to put your finger on exactly why you are bothered, and that's okay. Feel free to explore things further with him if you wish, just to make sure you're not being paranoid or bringing an unfortunate past experience with a pathological liar into the present. Your intuition is only a starting point for finding out more about him—but it's a damn powerful one. Superpowerful, in fact.

The Good, the Bad, and the Truly Ugly

It seems a little shallow, cold-hearted even, to put potential partners into categories, and yet it's a really good method for fine-tuning your skills at finding a great guy. Date enough men and you'll be able to determine quickly whether he's a good guy or one of the butt-ugly ones. Of course, there are shades of gray between these categories—a good guy can have a couple of bad habits that give you pause—but, in general, men fall into one of three distinct groups: good, bad, and ugly.

As Good As It Gets

Many women complain about the fact that they can't find a good guy, and I completely agree that they are few and far between. However, I also believe that many women simply don't notice a good guy even when he's right in front of her face.

Look, this isn't brain surgery. There are simply things that a good guy does right from the very start that make it pretty obvious he's one of the good ones. Some examples are:

- He listens to you and to others. He's genuinely interested in those around him and in what they have to say. Translation: he's not a self-centered narcissistic jerk who demands to be the center of attention.

- He has good manners. While not overly chivalrous (that would be irritating), the good guy makes an effort to open doors. He gives up his seat on the bus for the ninety-year-old woman with a cane while all the bad guys look the other way and mumble into their cell phones. At the park, he picks up his dog's poop and takes a minute to kick the soccer ball around with the kids (as opposed to the creep who parks his butt on the bench so he can check out all the hotties that walk by).

- He has a good job, decent friends, and a nice place to live. Good guys basically have it together. They may not be living on Park Avenue and driving a $50K luxury sedan, but they work hard to make sure the basics are covered. Contrast this with the artist types who freeload off everyone around them rather than take responsibility for supporting themselves (or their children).

- He's sexy and handsome, but in a shy, big-hearted kind of way. He doesn't spend all day in front of the mirror, but he does take care of his looks and is generally well groomed. He is likely to consider himself okay-looking rather than extremely good-looking. His low-key self-confidence makes you feel comfortable when you're around him.

> "I don't think there is a particular type of man that is better or easier for single moms to date, but I can say that older men and those with children of their own tend to gravitate to single moms. Younger guys seem to not want the burden of a child. The men without kids that show interest tend to be one of two types: those who wish your child were their own and rescuers who feel they can save you from the misery of a life alone and the hardships that come along with it."
>
> —Lee, 29, Seattle

Ultimately, it's best to keep an open mind with any man. Although you may find that a certain "type" works better for you as an individual, it's clear to me that there isn't one type that works for single moms in general. In other words, to each her own.

> "I think I'd look for men with kids, older men. I went on a blind date with a childless twenty-seven-year-old not long ago and we were on different planets when it came to life experience. Nice guy, but not a chance it would ever work. If I date someone again, he will be at least thirty-five and hopefully have a kid or two."
>
> —Carrie, 37, Boston

Bad Dog

You may have heard that it's inappropriate to call your children "bad," as in "you're being a bad boy today," because it indicates a judgment of their worth as a person rather than of their behavior alone. But, if you're talking about a boy of say, thirty, then I think it's just fine to call him "bad." "Asshole" is okay, too. He's an adult; he can take it. Besides, if he is indeed one of the bad ones, he deserves to hear it.

So, how do you know? Unfortunately there often seems to be a direct correlation between how good a guy is in bed and how bad he is out of it. This isn't always true—there are plenty of good guys who are great in the sack—but bad boys tend to be sluts who sleep around a lot so they have more opportunities to perfect their sexual skills. Sadly, by the time you find this out, you've already slept with him, you're attached, and you want more of it. So try really hard to get a fix on whether a man you like is trouble before you slide in between his five-hundred-thread-count Calvin Klein sheets. Here are some clues:

- He's rude. He forgets to call, and often he's late or cancels at the last minute.

- He talks about other women a lot. Old girlfriends, ex-wives, coworkers, the lady who delivers his mail—he knows all their names and what color their eyes are.

- He's showy. His car, clothes, apartment, and even his friends all look like they leaped off the pages of the latest issue of *Maxim* magazine. This guy has never met a trend he didn't like, and if you aren't as *au courant* as he, he'll make sure you know it.

• If he has kids, they're on the outskirts of his radar. Sure, he pays his child support every month, but he bitches about it plenty. If attending his son's soccer game means he can't sit courtside at the Lakers game, he's resentful as hell. He may even ask you to go to his kid's soccer game in his place—after all, he just loves the Laker Girls.

• Sex with him is more like a porn-movie shoot than an intimate encounter with someone you want to know better, and your first tryst with him includes a whole range of positions, methods, and gyrations. He acts as if he has only one chance to try every move with you, so he crams it all in (forgive the unfortunate pun) in a single evening. This is a pretty good sign he doesn't plan on there being a second time, so he's trotting out his whole repertoire at once.

"A single mom doesn't want to just date some hot stud. Okay, so maybe I want to. Okay, I definitely do. But if the opportunity somehow arose, my 'inner mom responsibility' would remind me that what I really need is someone who is mature, responsible, a family man. So single moms tend to cut through all the fluff and fun, and even if they don't admit it, look for the 'let's settle down and raise my kid right' kind of guy."

—Julie, 21, Boston

DOING THE LOVE LIMBO:
HOW LOW CAN YOU GO?

I will be the first to admit that before I got wise, I got down in the gutter. I dated losers with a capital L. Why? Part of it was that there just seemed to be a lot more of them around, and part of it was that I was often duped. For instance, I dated one guy who claimed to be a professional writer when in fact he spent the majority of his time on less noble pursuits. Then there was the freeloading "antiques dealer" (in other words, he liked yard sales and had a lot of junk in storage) who barged into my life, drained my savings, then hightailed it back home to mommy and daddy. While writing this book, I have heard many horror stories from single moms who stooped *way* too low in order to have a boyfriend. Dating beneath us isn't unique to single moms—plenty of childless women will admit to having done the same thing—but for us, the stakes are higher. I've also spoken with single moms who were actually thankful for having swum in the cesspool of lousy men, because now they know how pointless, draining—even dangerous—it can be, and they are never going in there again. Indeed, the best part of doing the love limbo is that once you've stooped as low as you can, there's nowhere for you to go but up.

Ugly Is As Ugly Does

There are two kinds of ugly: inside and outside. Men that are repulsive on the inside are tricky. Their exterior may make your knees weak, which means you're apt to overlook their corroded interior. Keep an eye out for some of these traits typical of guys who are ugly on the inside:

- He hates his mother. Sure, there are bad moms out there, and they can do a lot of damage. But that's what therapy is for. And forgiveness. And understanding. Yet this guy would rather continue to loathe his mother than do something about it. I personally find this trait to be repulsive.

- He's a skinflint. There are guys out there who are cheaper than Mr. Krabs on *SpongeBob SquarePants.* This trait is even more nauseating in men who make plenty of money, then turn up their nose at the homeless woman begging on the street corner next to her emaciated dog.

- He's a closet misogynist. A surefire way to spot a woman hater? Look for guys who go out of their way to tell how much they "love women." Or how "liberated" they are. No doubt he'll be spouting this stuff while he orders you to fetch him another drink. Stay away.

- He's depressed and completely in denial about it. Could there be anything less attractive than a man who hates his life and pretty much everything else, too? If you find yourself infatuated with a total downer, maybe *you're* not taking enough Zoloft.

Looks aren't everything. I've dated pale-faced men, not-so-tall men, and guys with more hair on their legs than on the top of their heads. So I'd be the last person to judge a man on looks alone.

However, there are places where one simply must draw the line. There are some physical characteristics that are so utterly unappealing they cause you to sprint out the door, even if he's the nicest guy in the world.

Here are a few of the uglies that should really turn you off:

- Excessive back hair. Come on, guys! We shave our legs and our armpits. We endure menstrual pain, labor contractions, and fifteen or so years of perimenopausal insanity before the ordeal of menopause finally arrives. We pluck our brows, plump up our lips, and have our pubic hair waxed so we can look like a porn star. And you can't endure five minutes of sheer torture while some chick rips that rug off your back? *Please.*

- Visible nose hair. There is a tool for this, you can find it the drugstore, and it doesn't cost much. Go get one, or get outta my way.

- Bad breath. Kissing is a life-sustaining activity, second only to breathing. If you're putting out fumes that are guaranteed to make a woman pass out, keep your tongue safely inside your mouth.

"Be incredibly picky about who you choose to date. No mercy dates or going out with someone you know you aren't going to be into— that is not a good reason to take time away from your kid (or yourself!). And don't waste time on people who don't understand what it means to have a small child."

—Carrie, 37, Boston

A SINGLE GUY ON THE PROS AND CONS OF DATING SINGLE MOMS

Nobody's perfect—including us. When guys date us, they get the entire package, including our children and sometimes even an ex, so it's important to remember that any man who decides to date us is taking on a lot. Here is one guy's opinion of some of the positives—and pitfalls—of being romantically involved with a single mom.

His Story: "I've dated five single moms, which translates to "slept with." I had serious relationship expectations with two, and the other three were flings that lasted a month or less. My first single mom experience was when I was twenty-eight and she was thirty-eight with a six-year-old son."

What Worked: "Hot sex! I believe single moms have had some practice at this whole sex thing and are willing to go above and beyond to please their partner. Why? I have two theories. Maybe sex with their ex-husband became routine, and they are not wasting any more time with the same old sex. Single moms want to experience their fantasies and get what they want out of a relationship. This one might sting a little, but I thought that a couple of single moms I dated might have been eager to please me sexually because they wanted me to fill that missing husband/parent role. Having no children, I can only imagine that parenting is a tough job, and sharing the responsibility would make life a lot easier for the single mom."

What Didn't Work: "Would I be labeled selfish or chauvinistic to think that I should come first in a relationship? I learned that when dating a single mom, I'd have to accept all of her into my life, including her kids, and I wasn't prepared to share my single mom's love and attention. It seemed as if everything had to be planned around the kids—which movie to go to, what and when to eat, scheduling around bedtimes and daycare. Some women will say, 'Oh, grow up and be more responsible,' but being spontaneous and doing adult things is exciting and keeps the relationship fresh, right?"

The End: "The last single mom I dated missed her period in the second month of our relationship and I quickly found myself discussing parenting responsibilities and 'how wonderful it would be to have another child.' We drove straight to the drugstore to buy a pregnancy test. The negative results couldn't pull that relationship from the flames of failure. How could anyone make such a life-changing decision with only two months of relationship history? Maybe she thought another child was a way to keep me, or maybe she wanted another child-support check. After that, I swore off single moms."

His Advice: "Be up front with your intentions and the fact that you have a child. Everyone wants to feel wanted and important in a relationship. Make the effort—I know it's difficult—to put your partner first and he will feel important enough to make you and your kids his priority."

—Sean, 34, Seattle

Where the Boys Are

Now that you know how to sort out the good guys from all the rest, where on earth can you find them?

Everywhere. Every time you step out of the house, be prepared to embrace the unexpected. It's okay to have a strategy, and if you're serious about finding a partner, you do have to make a consistent effort. But don't forget that many happily attached women say they met someone when they least expected it.

Still, there's nothing wrong with helping the hand of fate. When it comes to creating opportunities to meet eligible, appropriate, and interesting men, consider activities and places where you can get something besides a hot date out of your efforts, whether it's new friendships, skills, exercise, or whatever. That way, if you come up empty-handed on the romance front, at least you have something to show for your investment of time and energy. Here's my list of good places to meet good guys, based on my personal experience, input from other single moms, and just plain common sense:

- Classes
- Clubs
- Parks
- Estate sales
- Political rallies
- Hiking trails
- Dog parks
- Festivals
- Farmers' markets
- Video rental stores
- Church or spiritual centers
- Film festivals
- Airports
- Airplanes
- Coffee shops
- PTA meetings
- Bookstores
- Yard sales
- Museums
- Art gallery walks

- Neighborhood events
- Community centers
- Your kids' daycare

These venues are not specifically designed for meeting members of the opposite sex—which is exactly the point: the pressure is off. And since single moms have so little leisure time, you're more apt to simply enjoy yourself rather than focus on the hunt, which of course ends up getting you more attention than if you went out looking for it.

In fact, many of the places that are specifically designed to help you find your soul mate are my least favorite methods for meeting great guys. Some examples:

- The Internet (There are some exceptions. See "Don't Get Caught in the Net")

- Dating services (these are generally overpriced and underperforming—hey, that sounds like someone I dated once!)

- Bars (do I even need to say this?)

- Blind dates set up by friends desperate to see you married off to *anyone*

"I meet eligible men everywhere when my children are not in tow. When I do have my children with me, I tend to meet them at the park, at the grocery store, or at a restaurant or coffee shop. Men seem hesitant to approach single moms unless it is in a very

public place and in a manner that could not be construed as inap-
propriate."

—Lee, 29, Seattle

If you're burned out on bookstores and the only guys you meet at the video store spend way too much time in the porn section, feel free to think outside the box—*way* outside the box:

- Funerals (who among us doesn't look hot in black?)

- Courtrooms (lots of cute lawyers around)

- Homeless shelters (hopefully you'd hook up with some adorable soup kitchen volunteer as opposed to one of the residents)

- A seminar on how to write a will (hey, at least you know he's a guy who plans ahead and actually has something to leave behind)

- Tantric sex seminar (maybe his partner will be a no-show)

DON'T GET CAUGHT IN THE NET

When online, people pretend to be things they are not. They can say things they don't really mean with few or no consequences, and many of the men are only looking to get laid. Indeed, online dating sites aren't that different from your standard meat market, only instead of the patrons being intoxicated with alcohol, they are high on the freedom, immediacy, and anonymity of the Internet. Both in a bar and on the Internet, people seem a lot cuter, smarter, and nicer than they really are (in a bar, this is because you're a bit buzzed; online, it's because you're dazzled by their ghostwritten bio and expertly retouched or decades-old photograph).

Despite all this, I continue to meet many single mothers who are absolutely enchanted by the Internet dating scene, and for some very understandable reasons. For one thing, you don't have to hire a sitter in order to interact with men. As Dr. Pepper Schwartz says, "Where else can you go looking for guys at eleven o'clock at night, and you don't have to leave the house?" You can get some much-needed attention, flirt with abandon, and even get your comatose libido resuscitated, all just by moving your mouse. But virtual romance also raises hopes, creates expectations, sucks up your time, and ultimately increases the number of hours you spend in isolation—which is already a problem for many single moms.

Many moms crow about how many men they have met on these sites and how many dates they've gone out on that otherwise would never have happened. However, when I've probed deeper, many of these women will admit that they wish the majority of those dates had never happened. Remember girls, it's *quality*, not quantity that matters. The old adage about kissing a lot of frogs is still true—the more men you meet, the more likely you are to find one that's worth keeping—but the sheer abundance of toads swimming around on the Internet can be a disadvantage. My highly subjective advice? Resist the temptation to become an Internet dating addict. Consider matching services that focus on compatibility rather than superficial qualities, such as www.true.com. Or visit sites where you have at least some familiarity with the members, such as classmates.com. And a new site, www.singleparentlovelife.com, aims to avoid the meat-market approach of some websites and "caters to the unique needs of single parents." Still, if you feel compelled to surf the dime-a-dozen Internet dating sites out there that are not single-parent specific, do so with care. And keep an eye out for sharks.

Mission Accomplished

Obviously being a superhero when it comes to love is damn hard work. Is it worth it, you ask? Why not just be an ordinary schlub who makes mistakes, goes out with bad guys, gets her heart broken, then starts the whole pointless cycle all over again?

First of all, you are not ordinary. You are a mother. This in itself is extraordinary. Second, you're tired of dating the wrong kinds of men—otherwise, you wouldn't be reading this book. And finally, all the effort is worth it because *you're* worth it. If you don't agree, go back and reread Chapter One. Otherwise, you're ready to embark on that most desired and, at the same time, dreaded event: a first date with someone you really like. And you thought *getting* a date was the hard part.

chapter five

Disaster

Prevention

Plan

FROM BABYSITTERS TO BABY TALK,

DATING IS FRAUGHT WITH PERIL

FOR THE SINGLE MOM

"I love being a single mom.
But it's definitely different when you're dating."
—Brooke Burns, actress

"Preparedness prevents peril."
—Chinese proverb

Congratulations. If you're taking time out of your insane schedule to read this chapter, you must actually have a date lined up or maybe just the chance of having some hot sex. Either way, you have an opportunity to spend some time in the company of another human being who won't ask you to bring him a snack, kiss his boo-boo, or wipe his derriere. (Come to think of it, I've had grown men ask me to do all of the above, either literally or figuratively.)

No doubt you're excited. But before you run out and spend your hard-earned money to get a bikini wax, buy sexy lingerie, get a new haircut, or have an astrology reading to see if you and this total stranger are going to get hitched someday—before you do *any* of those things—make sure you are really ready for this.

You should know by now that dating as a mom isn't at all like it was when you were a responsibility-free young single woman. Back then, the biggest thing you had to worry about was to eat something at dinner to soak up all those free cocktails, so you wouldn't throw up on the guy later that night.

Now there are a slew of minefields you must anticipate and step gingerly around in order to have a great hot date. So, as we so often say to our progeny, pay attention! These irritating obstacles can turn a potentially romantic or lustful evening into a night you might wish you could forget.

Mother's Little Helper

Let's start with the one constant every single mother must deal with if she is to date: the babysitter, a.k.a., the person on whom you depend in order to have a life but whom you secretly resent and/or have issues with for a whole bunch of reasons, not the least of which is because she's so damned expensive.

Babysitters, nannies, caregivers, call them what you will. Just be sure and call them way in advance or the only place you'll be going Saturday night is to bed. Very early. Alone.

How could your babysitter possibly sabotage your love life? That depends on what kind of sitter you have. I've found that babysitters often resemble characters from movies, so it might help to reference a few flicks as we strive to understand the critical role they play in your ability to go on a date without losing your mind.

THE HAND THAT ROCKS THE CRADLE

This nanny is young, beautiful, has a great body and secretly gets off on getting your man's attention, and she may even want him all for herself. And while she may not be planning to knife you in your sleep to take over your life (who would want to take over the life of a single mom?), she *will* go out of her way to flirt with just about any guy that walks through your front door. Even if she's great with the kids, your best bet is to show her the door, and fast, unless you want to start the evening more insecure and stressed out than you already are.

UNCLE BUCK

Whether male or female, this sitter is as real as it gets. Think Wal-Mart wardrobe, fast-food bags on the counter, and a rather unappealing tendency to pass gas, which the little ones, of course, find most amusing. Unfortunately, this may all be a bit too real for your potential paramour, who might wonder how you could leave your precious offspring in the care of such an irresponsible slob. The short answer is that she was available and you could afford her, but hopefully the truth is something closer to, "She's the best sitter I've ever had. She's studying to be an emergency room nurse and the kids just love her." The bottom line is that he may see your choice in caregivers as a reflection on you. So if you can, forgo the low-rent version, at least for the first few dates. But do not, by any means, go to the other extreme and hire a Rebecca De Mornay look-alike.

KRAMER VS. KRAMER, MRS. DOUBTFIRE, LOOK WHO'S TALKING

I've lumped these flicks into a single very dicey category: the Guy Babysitter. It doesn't matter if that guy is your ex-husband, an out-of-work (but cute) friend, or a man disguised as a frumpy woman. The truth is that upon entering your home for the first time, your date will immediately feel that he has competition. This will make him cranky and you will be made to feel guilty, even if you've never had the pleasure of "doing the babysitter."

Despite the tremendous progress we've made over the last forty years in terms of gender roles (well, the mediocre progress at least), most men still find it strange, and even sexually threatening, to date a woman who has a man in her house, even if he's just the hired help. Maybe he's afraid the sitter will be sniffing your panties while you two are at the movies and he'd rather reserve that little activity for himself. Who knows? The point is that if you must have a man watch the kids, make sure he's either unattractive or obviously not attracted to women. Then, in the latter case, the only obstacle you'll have to deal with is keeping him from hitting on your date. (Another plus of having a gay babysitter: No one has better gaydar than a gay man, so if you want to make sure your date is firmly ensconced on the hetero team, have your sitter check him out.)

> "Babysitters! It's very easy for most guys to meet for coffee. If I have a babysitter come to the house, it means I have to pay her for three hours time. If she babysits at her house, there is extra driving, packing juicy cups, snacks, and so on. All for a lousy cup of coffee!"
> —Stephanie, 32, New Hampshire

Of course, the most important thing is to hire a babysitter who will take excellent care of your children. If you can also find one who is plain, soft-spoken, responsible, neat, and, well, *normal*, so much the better, particularly when it comes to getting your evening off to a smooth start. (Actually, if you find one with all of those qualities, call me—I want her number.)

Silence Is Golden

Would you introduce a man you barely know to your mother or father on a first date? Of course not. Then why do some single moms insist on trotting out their children on such an occasion? Perhaps it's a matter of pride—your children are your greatest achievement after all—but it's a risky move and perhaps a little selfish on your part. If your unconscious goal is to make this guy fall in love with your family, you might as well introduce him to a snarling 120-pound Rottweiler because, believe me, it will scare the bejesus out of him to meet the clan when he barely knows you. Rather than becoming enamored with your children, no matter how adorable they are, he may instead think that if he follows through with this dinner date he could end up supporting the lot of you for the rest of his life. It's not rational, but that's how some guys think.

Give him a chance to get to know you as an individual before integrating him with the rest of the crowd. After all, not all dates lead to second, third, and fourth dates, so why confuse your kids by parading some strange guy in front of them? And why spook him until you're sure he can handle it?

Having him meet your kids is probably just plain inappropriate until you've been on several dates, he's expressed an interest in meeting them, and you're absolutely certain he's not some cretin with a secret past life as a priest who was mysteriously asked to leave the clergy or a wife beater currently out on bail.

OUT OF THE MOUTHS (AND PENISES) OF BABES

I once had a date arrive early, and my nanny ushered him into the nursery without giving me any warning. There I stood in my bathrobe, my hair wrapped in a towel (thankfully, I had already applied my makeup), changing my son's diaper while his twin brother methodically pulled the stuffing out of a teddy bear and crammed it into his mouth. My date was decent enough to realize he'd caught me off guard and, in an effort to help me relax, he cooed at my boy and tickled his tummy while I slid a diaper beneath him and attempted to make small talk. Just before I was able to fasten his diaper, my little angel shot a fountain of pee directly at my date, hitting him square in the eye and splattering his crisp, white J. Crew shirt. He waited a moment—in shock no doubt—before cussing up a storm, while my baby stared up at him in confusion. "Well, you shouldn't have tickled him while he was having his diaper changed," I protested weakly. He smirked at me, grabbed a burp cloth, and wiped his eye and shirt. Then he walked out of my house without a single word.

I know single moms who have been absolutely mortified by the words and actions of their youngsters in front of their dates. The classic faux pas is a toddler asking innocently, "Are you my new Daddy?" upon which the guy typically fumbles around for a response, and you suddenly find some reason to leave the room. Or your date arrives just as the kids are engaged in a nasty fight. Food and toys are flying, everyone's crying, and inside you're dying. "They're hardly ever like this," you say, as your date eyes you with extreme suspicion. In the next beat, he's nearly knocked out by the metal dump truck that was just tossed at his head.

You see my point. Kids will be kids no matter how great your date may be. So do yourself and the guy a favor: child-proof your evening from the get-go. Keep the little ones a safe distance from your date until you're on your way out the door.

"Don't just blurt out that you have a kid when you first meet a guy, or even on a first date. Let him get to know you a little first, and then mention it appropriately in conversation. You're not hiding it, you're just giving him a glimpse of you as 'sexy woman,' not 'mom.' Then, once he knows, if he does hightail it, you'll know it was because of your kid, not you. In that case, you don't need him anyway."

—Julie, 21, Boston

Mis-Manners

If you manage to get out of the house without making your date flee like a man with his hair on fire, the good news is, the possibilities are endless. The bad news is, the possibilities are endless.

For instance, it's entirely possible that you'll dazzle your date with your ability to speak fluent Spanish to the valet guy, or that your carefully chosen little black dress will reveal just enough cleavage to make him want to see more of you (literally). Or perhaps, in a fit of spontaneity, you suggest that you skip the movie and go bowling after dinner, whereupon you throw a perfect strike as your skirt billows up behind you, a la Marilyn Monroe, offering him just a glimpse of your gartered thigh.

However, it's more likely that your evening will go something like this: You are so stressed out and exhausted from trying to get ready while the kids follow you around like Labrador puppies, the sitter showing up late, and the big fat zit that just sprouted on your chin that you can't form basic sentences, let alone speak a foreign language. Plus, your back hurts so bad from bending over to pick up kids, laundry, and toys that you can't seem to get comfortable sitting at a restaurant—forget about physical activity of any kind (yes, including *that* kind).

So what's it gonna be? Mission impossible, or anything's possible? The answer, of course, is up to you.

Much of it depends on how well you have prepared for the evening. Here, then, is a checklist of items to arrange before the big date:

- If it's a weeknight, leave work early. Take some time to yourself to chill out—go for a walk, get a manicure, or take a nap.

- Get the kids something extra, even if it's only a special snack, so they'll have something to take their minds off of you and where you're going that evening.

- Ask the sitter to come at least an hour before your date is due to arrive. That way, you're not trying to transition the kids to someone else's care while your date stands idly by feeling awkward as your babies cling to your legs. Plus, your caregiver can keep them occupied so you can get ready in peace. It's worth the extra ten bucks, believe me.

- If you're really nervous, pour yourself a glass of wine. Put on some sexy music and get yourself beautiful. Hopefully you knew this date was coming up, so you've been thinking about which outfit you might wear and you won't have to tear your closet apart looking for the perfect thing.

- If you're particularly attracted to this guy, and it's been a while since you've gotten any, take a page from the movie *There's Something about Mary*. You know, the scene where Ben Stiller masturbates before he goes out on his date with Cameron Diaz. Leave out the part where evidence of the deed ended up dangling from his earlobe. Of course, we don't have to worry about that now, do we? Oh, and make sure you take care of your needs where you're certain you won't be disturbed by the little ones, if such a place exists. Don't underestimate the value of a good lock on the bedroom or bathroom door.

- Pour yourself another (small) glass of wine, but only if you also eat a light snack. Answering the door drunk won't impress him much.

- Check the contents of your purse and take out any potentially offensive items (see "Handbag Hell," right).

Once you're all dolled up, take a few minutes to visit with your children. If one of them starts to whine and complain about you going out without her, refuse to get worked up. Simply make it the sitter's problem, kiss her goodnight, and close the bedroom door.

Find something useful to do while you wait for your date to arrive. I like to call a girlfriend and chat until the doorbell rings or pop a Xanax (kidding!).

You can also simply meet him outside your home, which works particularly well for a first or second date. After that, he might think you've got something to hide (like a husband), so eventually you'll have to invite him to your home. When that time comes, allow him a very brief glance around your place, grab your purse and coat, and get the hell out of there. Otherwise, the kids are bound to break out of their room to get a look at the guy or cause some scene just as you're feeling really in control of things.

Handbag Hell

Do not, I repeat, *do not*, go out on a date without first purging your purse of all child-related things: sippy cups, pacifiers, scribbled drawings, half-eaten graham crackers, crumpled Band-Aids, boxes of raisins, baby wipes, and obnoxious beeping dime-store toys. Believe it or not, this kind of stuff freaks guys out. If he were to spot a small handgun in your bag, he'd be just fine with it, but pull out an empty juice box and he's instantly reminded that you have this whole other messy life at home. Eventually, after you've been dating a while, seeing the detritus of your daily existence shouldn't alarm him—and if it does, toss him faster than a day-old diaper. But until you reach that point, take only the essentials out on the town: a bit of makeup, your cell phone, some cash, your ID, some condoms, and a gorgeous smile. After all, this is supposed to be fun, remember?

> *"It's hard to explain to guys that you are on a tight schedule, so if he wants to go out, you need some time to plan, time to line up a babysitter. I once dated a single dad who had a similar schedule, and it was great to find someone who got it."*
>
> —Alison, 39, San Francisco

Baby Talk

As a single mom, it's easy to go for long periods of time without a date. This means you get rusty, and you can become stuck in mom mode. Then, when you do get the opportunity for a night on the town, you tend to go a little overboard. For instance, since you haven't had an adult conversation in so long, you may hang onto your date's every word, looking fascinated when he tells you that he had his oil changed that day. And then he'll think you're either playing him or totally insane. Or you might start talking to him like he's one of your children simply out of habit. Before you know it, you're cutting his meat into itsy-bitsy pieces so he doesn't choke—and he's looking for exit signs.

Here's a tip: hit the mute button! Let him do the talking at first. Focus on what he's saying, and before you know it you're a woman again—a grown-up out on a date—and the mom side of you is taking a breather.

Now that you're more relaxed, you have a chance to let him get to know you a little bit. But before you open your yap, remember that certain topics are simply off limits, particularly on a first date. Therefore, do not talk about:

- How hard it is to be a single mom
- How great it was to give birth
- How horrible it was to give birth
- How much it costs to hire a babysitter
- Why your ex is such an ass
- How much you wish you were married
- How happy you are that you aren't married
- How much weight you gained after giving birth
- What happened at your Mommy and Me outing last week
- How cute, smart, obnoxious, irritating, and wonderful your kids are

Unfortunately, this might leave very little for you to talk about.

Here's some simple but foolproof advice: relax and be yourself. I'm talking about the cool, cute, fun, and interesting you—not the exhausted, stressed, cynical, needy you. Try to remember what you were like before you became a parent. What interested you? Besides raising children, what are you goals? Where would you like to travel one day? The list of suitable dinner conversation topics is endless. The key is to keep reminding yourself that you're great, you're beautiful, and there's more to you than just being a mom. Even if it's the role you're most proud of (and it should be), it's not *all* you are.

YOU ARE ONE HOT MAMA

Remember when going on a date was something to be thrilled about? When, even though you were nervous, you were also hopeful and excited? In those days, it probably didn't occur to you that you might not be worth dating at all.

As single moms, we can sometimes feel like someone is doing us a huge favor just by taking us to dinner and a movie. That's because we feel like if we were really worth dating, we'd be married, and life would be perfect, and we wouldn't need to go through this horrible ordeal time and time again. For some reason, we might feel that (to quote from *Wayne's World*) "We're not worthy."

Hold on, sister. That feeling of being a second-class citizen has no place on a date (or anywhere else in your life, for that matter). Taking low self-esteem out with you for an evening is like wearing your prettiest, most flattering little black dress and bringing along a garish, altogether mismatched and totally wrong handbag just because you've had it for such a long time and it holds all your stuff. And besides, you ask, who will notice? *After all, I'm wearing this great dress.*

Well, he'll notice, and deep down, so will you.

Go back and reread Chapter One. Refuse to buy into the stereotype of the single mom as some kind of lonely loser! Remember that you are doing something incredibly important.

You are raising children, loving them, creating their future with every fiber in your being. And after this evening has ended, you get to go home to them, kiss their little heads, and watch them sleep. And when you wake up, they will be there, and they will love you, and you will love them. That is yours. Just remember that when you start to feel unsure of yourself as a desirable, valuable woman. Remember that the only person who can judge you is you, and chances are you do plenty of that already.

Until you feel like you deserve to date not just a decent guy but a great guy, and that *he's* lucky you've carved out some time in your insane life to spend with him, until you really, really believe it, you're better off not dating at all. Instead, stay home, open a good Cabernet, and watch a movie. Maybe even *Wayne's World*.

Good Night, Sweet Prince

You've managed to get through dinner without incident. Your after-dinner walk was actually kind of romantic. And now you're sitting in his car outside of your house wondering what the hell to do.

One of the blessings (or curses, depending on your libido) of single motherhood is that simply hopping in the sack with your date is rarely an option. These things must be planned. The decision to end the evening with a bang (so to speak) or a whimper, or something in between, should be made earlier—before dessert arrives, but at the very latest, before you pull into your driveway.

Basically, you have two choices. If you're very attracted to him physically but don't really care if you ever see him again after tonight, by all means, go back to his place, rip his clothes off, and treat yourself to another kind of dessert—one that burns calories instead of piles them directly onto your thighs.

If you choose to go this route, make sure your date understands the rules of engagement:

1. No glove, no love (I'm talking condoms, of course).

2. Postcoitus, you (or he) must leave posthaste. No sleepovers allowed. The last thing you want is to fall asleep accidentally and roll into your house at 6 A.M., or, worse yet, for your kids to find him in *your* bed the next morning.

3. No guilt—for either of you. Make sure he understands that this doesn't obligate him to call you again (or vice versa). However, if you genuinely like each other in bed and out, maybe there will be a round two. But be honest with yourself and him.

Your second option is to kiss your friend goodnight—you can even make out in his car, which is guaranteed to make you feel like a teenager again—and then exit gracefully. You'll want to pursue this course of action if you feel like there's something there—the chance for a real relationship developing or perhaps just a great friendship. The thing to remember is that this is your decision. It's your body, your family is inside that house, and ultimately it's your heart and your conscience that you want to protect, so don't let any man persuade you to have sex before you're ready. In fact, if he is really insistent that you rush things, it's pretty clear this guy sees you as a pit stop along the way to better things (and you, therefore, should view him the same way).

If you're in a hurry (perhaps you're reading this in the bathroom at the restaurant trying to decide what to do while your date wonders if you've ditched him), just play it safe: no sex. Kissing, fondling, teasing—why not? But until you're sure you can live with the consequences of doing the deed, keep your little black dress on.

> *"I need to be more picky about what to do when. Gone are the days of groping in the back of a Chevy. No more backyard trysts."*
> —Stephanie, 32, New Hampshire

The Dating Game

Clearly, dating can be complicated for single moms, but that doesn't mean it's impossible or that you shouldn't try. "There is no way to embrace life fully unless you enter it and you take the time to have a personal life," says Dr. Pepper Schwartz. "You need to understand not everyone is going to like you and you are not going to like everyone, but each experience will deepen your range of emotions and social interactions."

Indeed, with a little preparation, common sense, and the right attitude, you might find that dating can be a lot of fun. And lest you forget, if you never date, you'll never get to have sex, which of course brings with it a whole other set of challenges, which we'll discuss a bit later in Chapter Seven. Unless you're one of those naughty girls who went to the chapter on sex *first*.

chapter six

Kiddus Interruptus

HOW TO MAKE SURE YOUR CHILDREN

DON'T RUIN YOUR LOVE LIFE—

AND VICE VERSA

*"In the United States today, there is a
pervasive tendency to treat children as adults,
and adults as children. The options of children are
thus steadily expanded, while those of adults are
progressively constricted. The result is unruly
children and childish adults."*
—Thomas Szasz, Professor of Psychiatry Emeritus at the State
University of New York Health Science Center, Syracuse

*"Don't worry that children never listen to you;
worry that they are always watching you."*
—Robert Fulghum, author

You can learn a lot about love just by watching your children. Their trusting, openly emotional nature, their ability to express love (and strong dislike) with ease, their vulnerability, fear of abandonment, and need for affection—all of these things we adults can also experience when we are dating or seriously involved with someone. Perhaps that's why having a healthy love life as a single mom is often so difficult: our children's needs and desires tend to mimic our own, albeit on a familial level. Yet as every parent knows—or should know—your children always come first. Which means your needs always come last. Right?

Well, maybe not last, but certainly you're in second place. And the sooner you accept that your love life will have limits, most of which are determined by the demands of parenting, the sooner you'll be able to truly enjoy it, without the resentment, anger, and frustration many single moms experience when trying to balance child rearing and romance.

And while this book is mainly focused on how to improve your love life, if you don't first get your ducks in a row on the home front, it's safe to say you won't be having much of one. That's what this chapter is all about. I know this isn't nearly as fun as talking about men, makeup, and sex, but just remember: guys may come and go, but your children are yours forever. That's a really long time, and unless you want to spend it feeling guilty about how you messed up your kids with a series of romantic mishaps—or furious with them for causing your decade-long celibacy streak—then commit yourself to my "Nine steps to a kid-friendly love life" program.

The Good Old Days Are Over

Step one: Acceptance. Accepting your current situation means mourning a part of your past. Okay, maybe mourning is too strong a word, but at the very least you need to do some serious letting go of your old ways of doing things. For instance, spontaneity as it pertains to love and sex is, for the most part, no longer possible. As parents, our lives revolve around our children's schedules. So if the opportunity for a last-minute tryst comes along, remember that if it means you'll have to pick up your son at soccer practice twenty minutes late, he'll be scared and angry and you'll feel guilty, not to mention you'll probably get a speeding ticket on your way there as you try to make up for lost (libidinous) time. It's not fair to your kid or yourself, and as wonderful as it may feel to jump in bed for an unplanned quickie, ultimately it's not worth it.

Does this mean unexpected pleasures are a thing of the past? Well, that depends on how you define unexpected. The heady, anything-goes freedom you enjoyed when you were single and childless is gone, at least until your children are grown and out on their own. Trying to reclaim those days while also acting as a responsible parent is an exercise in futility. Instead, learn to be spontaneous *within* your planned events. Allow yourself to be flexible when you're on a date and to go with the flow rather than be completely regimented like you are in daily life. For example, if you and your paramour had planned to see a movie but you're feeling restless, suggest going for a stroll downtown and hitting a few bookstores instead. Or, instead of going to an overpriced restaurant for dinner, suggest cooking dinner at his place (assuming he doesn't also have kids at home) or going on a picnic in the park. Just do something different, unplanned, unexpected— anything that makes you feel like you can still do things on a whim. Just because you're a parent, your life doesn't have to be entirely predictable. However, make sure you're home on time or your kids (and your sitter) may display some spontaneous outbursts of their own.

> "It is difficult to have a successful love life as a single mom because alone time does not come easily. I used to be a very spontaneous person, but now every moment in my life has to be planned. My time without my children is more precious to me than gold, and I refuse to spend it with people whose company I may not enjoy."
>
> —Lee, 29, Seattle

Kill the Guilt before It Kills You

Step two: Entitlement. Single moms are perhaps the only people who can feel guilty about having sex and dating even when they aren't doing much of either. Even *thinking* about taking time and energy away from their children sends some moms into a frenzy of psychological self-flagellation. Ask these same moms if they felt bad when they went out on a date with their kids' father (when they were together) and the answer is usually no, or "not nearly as much." I believe guilt is one of the biggest obstacles to a successful love life for a single mom. Unfortunately, everyone from your mother to your sister to your coworkers to your kids can contribute to making you feel like crap about wanting to date, whether they are conscious of it or not.

The thing to remember about guilt is that if you don't get rid of it before you start dating, you'll enter the wonderful world of romance in a very half-assed way. Your ambivalence and worry about what you're doing will be written all over you. Men will pick up on it and run away like frightened little rabbits, because as I mentioned in a previous chapter, men hate guilt. They see it as contagious, and if you're feeling guilty, soon they will too, and they'd rather submit to a root canal without novocaine than be made to feel something is their fault (even when it clearly is not).

Understand you will always experience some degree of guilt whenever you are leaving your children, whether you're dashing off to work or on a much-needed weekend vacation by yourself. But when you take time away from your kids to date, your guilt is also laden with shame. We somehow feel that it's our fault we're single moms, and so we need to deny ourselves the pleasures of sex, love, and romance. We are martyrs of the first order.

Before you start dating, you simply must kill the guilt that goes along with it. Here's a great way to get started: Sit down and figure out how many hours per day you devote to your children and other family members (parents, grandparents, siblings, or whomever). This figure should include the hours you spend earning a living so that you can feed, clothe, and house your kids. Include the time you spend grocery shopping, cleaning, running errands, and so on, for these things, too, are all a part of being a good mom. Even the time you spend sleeping counts, because if you didn't sleep, you couldn't do any of the above. Then jot down how many hours you spend on yourself and your needs. I'd venture to guess the ratio is something like twenty-four hours to . . . none. (One friend of mine who went through this exercise actually found she was about two hours in the hole every day.)

When you look at it in black and white, you should start to feel pretty darn entitled to putting a few hours into your column. It doesn't matter how you use "your" time; that's your business and no one else's. The point is that a portion of the week should be set aside for you, and anytime your kids get in a huff about you not being immediately available to them for a few hours Saturday night, just whip out your handy-dandy Mommy the Magnificent chart and point out all the time you spend taking care of them.

Children, in fact, are perhaps our greatest source of guilt when it comes to dating. They are used to being the center of your universe, and when this changes, even a little, they are outraged or, at the very least, they get pouty. You can try to make them understand that having a life of your own makes you a happier, better mother. If they aren't buying that argument, feel free to ignore them. This is hard, I know. But if you allow your kids to dictate whether you can enjoy the company of men, you will end up resenting them for it, and that will do more damage to your relationship with them than spending a limited time away each week.

Finally, a great way to kill the guilt is to make sure you have reliable babysitters that your children like and that the household is in order and things are calm when you decide to go out. This is easier said than done, but when I'm on a date, I am much more able to enjoy myself if I know the kids are in safe hands and they are having fun.

If these techniques don't work, your guilt may be the result of unresolved issues surrounding the absence of a father, limited financial resources, or too much time spent in Catholic school. If you must feel guilty about these things until you have spent enough time in therapy working them out, then go right ahead, but don't let it prevent you from feeling entitled to an active romantic life.

Are Your Kids Ready . . . or Not?

Step three: Assessment. Even if you're ready to get out there, your kids may not be. This can be difficult to determine, particularly if they are really young and not yet able to communicate their feelings clearly. Of course, an inability to communicate might apply to teenagers as well, who may be uncomfortable seeing their mom in dating mode. So how do you tell how your kids are feeling, and what can you do about it once you know?

Some of this is common sense. If you are freshly divorced or separated from your kids' father, simply assume they will be less than happy to see you with a new guy. And guess what? They may be right—it might be too soon. Before you resort to telling them that mommy knows best and dismissing their complaints out of hand, you may want to check your "Ex-Rating," in Chapter Two.

Assuming you've determined that you're healthy, stable, and rarin' to go, then you need to talk to your kids about your desire to date. Assure them that you're just exploring new friendships and relationships, which is what parents do once they are divorced or partners decide to live apart. Then, depending on how much you like a guy, you can decide how to proceed, including whether you want him to meet your children down the line and spend time with you and your kids together.

"I don't think you should hide your dates from your kids," Dr. Pepper Schwartz says. "If they are little, you don't want a parade of men coming through; however, you don't want them to hold onto this picture of someone who is still married to Daddy. You should start to disabuse them of that myth and fantasy. On the other hand, I don't think you should introduce your children to people who are meaningless in your life."

GROWING PAINS

It seems logical that romance would get easier as your children get older. After all, once they hit thirteen you cease to exist as far as they're concerned, right? Wrong. Conversely, one might assume that if your children are quite small, they are oblivious to your love life. Again, this simply is not the case.

In short, your children's age and maturity may have little to do with how they react to the introduction of a new boyfriend or even to your going out on the occasional date. I know single moms who have been alternately horrified and thrilled with how their kids have reacted. So since you can't always predict what they'll do, what can *you* do?

- Control how you react to their reactions. Even though they are getting emotional and upset and putting you very much on the defensive, you should try to stay calm and talk about the issues in a nonhostile way. This lessens the drama and puts your dating into the appropriate context. They should realize that your dating is not the end of the world and if you talk about it in a mature way, you'll understand each other better.

- Put your thinking cap on. When you're crazy about some guy and your hormones are in overdrive, you are more apt to be careless or dismissive of your kids' concerns. Try to hold your enthusiasm about your new squeeze in check—at least until you're alone—and instead be sensitive to your child's needs. If your child has abandonment issues from the breakup of your past relationship or the loss of a family member, you need to focus on her like a laser beam when talking things out. Don't allow yourself to be distracted by a man when your child needs you most.

- Have a laugh or two. Use this handy chart to get a handle on how your kids feel about you dating, from the time they're in diapers to the day they get their driver's license:

Ages 0–1: Change me, burp me, feed me, and rock me night and day and you can do anything you want in the five minutes a day you have left over.

Ages 2–4: I am the center of the universe and, most importantly, *your* universe. I fall down a lot and throw about ten tantrums a day. And I don't like sharing, especially you.

Ages 5–7: Where do babies come from? Are you and that man standing in the living room going to get married? Are you going to make a baby? Where is Daddy? Is he our new daddy? If you can answer all of these questions to my satisfaction, I will allow you to go out on a Saturday night. But just remember, I'm in charge!

Ages 8–10: Soccer on Mondays, drama class the next night, swim team on Fridays, and Girl Scouts this weekend. Oh, and can I invite six friends for a sleepover Saturday night? And when are you going to help me with my homework? Mom, I just don't think we have room in our lives for a boyfriend right now.

Ages 11–13: Mom, dating is for teenagers. You're too old. And you need to drop ten pounds. And why does that guy keep coming over? He doesn't even know how to use my Game Boy. What a loser!

Ages 14–16: Would you please quit borrowing my clothes? It's embarrassing. I don't care if you go out, but I am *not* staying with a babysitter—I'm old enough to stay home by myself. And if you're going to make out, please do it somewhere else—it totally grosses me out.

Ages 16 and above: Hey, I really like this one, Mom. Maybe we should go on a double date. I could bring my new girlfriend, Chloe. But you'll have to let me have my license back first.

No Revolving Doors

Step four: Be selective. There was one piece of advice I heard over and over again while researching and writing this book: do not introduce your children to a slew of different men, no matter how old your kids are. The dangers of doing this should be obvious, but just in case they aren't, let's review. Your children need to feel secure in their world and they need to be protected, both physically and emotionally, at all times. By parading a bunch of strangers in and out of your house, you are denying them the security they crave and are making their safety take a backseat to your desire to play the field. It's unfair, and it can damage your kids in the long run.

So, when *can* you bring a guy home to meet the kids? First of all, every situation is unique. I have heard from single moms who waited years—yes, years—before they felt secure enough in their relationship to introduce a boyfriend to her family. Personally, I think that if you have seriously dated someone for at least three months (there's something about the three-month mark—if a guy's been hiding something from you, if he's secretly a bully or he smokes pot when he says he's at the gym, these things tend to reveal themselves by month three) then you can perhaps arrange to introduce him to your kids at a neutral location. Go to the park, and he can drop by for a bit. Or arrange to eat dinner at a casual restaurant; that way, if things aren't going well, he can exit gracefully. But be sure you've talked to your kids about him first, and that they are ready and enthusiastic about meeting the person mommy goes out with on Saturday nights.

Or maybe you're spending Saturday nights in the sack with a guy that you don't ever intend to have a serious relationship with. These guys are sometimes referred to crassly as "fuck buddies" or the more genteel "friends with benefits." If it makes you feel good, go for it, but never, ever allow this person to cross your threshold and meet your family. You'll want to avoid talking about him to your children as well. If your kids want to know where you're going as you head out the door into orgasm land, it's okay to tell them a little white lie. Say you're going to exercise with a friend (well, you are, aren't you?).

> "Do not introduce your child to everyone you date. Children learn about relationships from those they see. If they see mom going out with a new guy every other week, how is this going to shape how they view dating relationships? It's going to cause some vicious cycles in their own dating patterns."
>
> —Maggie, 42, Denver

You Can't Clone Yourself

Step five: Set boundaries. When we're exhausted, which is most of the time, it's easy to take the path of least resistance with our children, the men we are involved with, and even our boss or co-workers. Sometimes we're just too tired to argue, to push back, and to protect ourselves and our interests. However, if you don't set limits with your kids and make them understand that you need to set aside some time and save *some* of your energy so that you can go out and enjoy new friendships, you may end up squandering the precious energy you have on endless arguments with your kids.

Set parameters that are easy to understand and simple to enforce. For example, you may decide that you will be going out on a date two evenings a month. (It might make sense to set this expectation with your kids even if you aren't currently dating someone. Use the time to have a date with yourself or your girlfriends so when you do find a man you want to spend time with, your kids are prepared.) Mark these nights on your calendar, show it to your children, and make it clear that nothing, short of them or you being sick, will make you change these plans.

You should also consider setting boundaries when you're at home. As any parent knows, the minute you get on the phone your kids seem to come out of nowhere to ask for a snack or tell you about their day at school. They know you are on the phone talking to that cute guy you really like, they see you waving your hands wildly trying to shush them, and yet they continue to make enough background noise to make the guy on the phone wonder if you're calling him from the zoo.

Let your kids know it's unacceptable to interrupt you when you're on the phone unless it's an emergency. Be sure to define "emergency" for them, even though they know perfectly well what it is. Otherwise they'll be tugging at your sleeve asking you why Christmas only comes once a year and if they can get a puppy. If they continue to get in your face just as you're trying to get to know somebody better through some intelligent conversation, turn the tables: Interrupt them the next time they watch *Sponge-Bob SquarePants*; or, if they're older, tell them you're going to listen in whenever they call up their friends—and that you will be taking notes. That should get them out of your face.

The bottom line is that your kids need to learn to share you. They already do this to a certain degree, allowing you to spend time at your job and with your friends, but now they have to learn to share mommy with a man, at least once in a while.

> *"It seems one relationship has to suffer for the other to thrive. Most men seem unable to wait patiently for you to put your children to bed, or deal with your child in the midst of a temper tantrum, or understand why your child can't have a rational conversation. On the other hand, your children don't understand the dynamics of a relationship, the boundaries and the work involved. Most young children are still in the 'me phase' and don't tolerate anyone taking attention away from them. It takes a special man to understand all of this."*
>
> *—Maggie, 42, Denver*

Safe Sex Requires
More Than Condoms

Step six: Be discreet. If you ever caught your own parents doing it when you were a kid, you know firsthand why you don't want your own children to find you naked and moaning with some guy on top of you. It doesn't matter if your children are two or twenty, it's simply embarrassing for everyone involved and can open a Pandora's box of questions from your kids about sex.

Reining in your sexual impulses can be really hard, especially if you haven't had sex in a while. On the other hand, you certainly don't want to jump in the sack too soon with someone you really like. So in this case, having kids provides single moms with a unique edge: their children serve as a kind of chastity belt, and while this may be frustrating, it can also be extremely helpful when you're just getting to know someone and you don't want to blow it.

However, hormones have a mind of their own, and you can only wait so long. When you decide you're ready to go all the way, as we were fond of saying in high school, I advise that you plan your first tryst very carefully. It doesn't really matter if you do it at his house, at your house, or in the dog house (okay, that might be a little weird), just make certain your kids are firmly ensconced elsewhere. Note that watching a movie downstairs in the family room doesn't count. They must be *off the premises*, either with a sitter, at school, with another family member, or on a playdate. This not only ensures they won't pop in unexpectedly and end up burdened for life with some Freudian nightmare of catching you in the act; knowing they are out of the house will also enable you to have a stress-free sexual encounter, during which you can truly relax and enjoy the lust and affection you've waited so patiently for.

When you're in an established relationship, at some point you'll need to figure out how to have a healthy sex life when your kids are around. You can't always get them out of the house, and quickies in the kitchen pantry get old after a while. This challenge is one faced by married couples as well, and many a parent has been caught in the act and struggled to make up some lame excuse for their strange behavior in the bedroom (strange to little children, repulsive to preteens, and all too understandable to teenagers). How you make your home impervious to coitus interruptus is up to you, but it helps to have kids who are sound sleepers. Barring that, you'll need to learn to have sex quietly, which we'll talk about in the next chapter. The main thing to remember is that your sex life is a private matter. Your children have nothing to do with it or say about it—and if, by not being discreet enough, you give them reasons to be curious or upset, then you really have no one to blame but yourself. So why go there? As any mom who's been put on the spot, pulling on her undies while her four-year-old points at her lover's manhood and asks, "What's that, Mommy?" can tell you, it's no place you ever want to be.

> *"Don't feel guilty about getting a sitter so you can have sex at some cheesy hotel. It's better that way. I swear, children subconsciously pick up on lovemaking even while they're sleeping . . . and inevitably interrupt it."*
>
> —Julie, 21, Boston

The Brady Bunch
Was Just a TV Show

Step seven: Put your family first. Bringing a new person into the safe, comfortable cocoon of your family is a big step for everyone: you, your kids, the family dog, your babysitter, oh, and the guy you're dating. It's an exciting and often fun-filled time, too, when you and yours can break free a bit from the cloistered environment of your daily lives spent mostly in the company of each other.

Still, you and your kids will enjoy the journey a lot more if you're confident you have your old familiar family unit to come home to. No doubt the dynamics of the family will change somewhat, but the core foundation of your children's lives—the routines, special traditions, and consistent parental guidance they are used to—should remain rock solid. Your children should be assured that although this new person is a part of their lives now, their life will remain very much the same. This is easier to accomplish when you're dating someone without kids. If your guy has children of his own, it's harder, because everything is more confusing and chaotic with more kids around. There's a temptation to simply toss everyone together and to start parenting as a unit. Shared parenting is probably a healthy way for things to evolve over time in a serious, long-term relationship, but until you're certain you're going to merge families, it's important that you and he agree that making sure all the children feel safe is the top priority. If you do this, your kids are much more apt to be supportive of your relationship instead of railing against it.

Your Family Is Not Weird

Step eight: Develop a support system. Many of the moms I heard from during the writing of this book spoke about being very sad and upset when their kids asked questions like "Why isn't our family like everyone else's?" or "Why can't we have a daddy? Can't you find one?"

It's not their fault. Our screwed-up society continues to foster the perception that a two-parent household is the Holy Grail, where the sun always shines, the children are happy, and the parents are in a loving relationship. We adults know that in many families, nothing could be further from the truth, but try telling that to an eight-year-old who is pining to have a man around to take him to Little League practice. It's heartbreaking to have to tell him that's just not possible sometimes. So, instead of telling him, show him: make friends with other single moms or single dads and get together for regular events. The more your kids see that there are many, many families without two parents living together under the same roof, the less they'll feel like outcasts. See the Additional Resources section at the back of this book for information on where you can find single parent support and social groups in your area.

Another way to put a positive spin on your situation is to point out the benefits of being part of a single-parent household. For instance, they don't have to see adults fighting or crying. (However, you'll also want to make it clear that not all parents fight, but many do, and you don't want to subject them to that—you'd rather wait for a good relationship.) You can also explain that by not having another person in your life full-time, you are free to focus more on them. Or mention that by not being stuck with a dad with problems, as a family, you have been given the opportunity to find a great man to become part of your lives.

Lastly, try to enlist the support of your children's father, if he is in the picture. Ask that he not sabotage your efforts to date and move on with your life, especially as it pertains to influencing the children one way or another about a particular guy. I realize some men will be unwilling to help you in this regard, but if you explain how much easier it would make life for your children—by eliminating confusion and minimizing conflict—he may be willing to support your efforts. And don't forget, there is always family counseling. If you are at an impasse with your kids and are arguing a lot about your relationship (or lack thereof) with a man, seek professional help.

Kids Are Blessings—in Disguise

Step nine: Remember the positives. By now, you may be thinking that having kids in the picture presents so many obstacles to dating that it's almost not worth it. It's true that having a family forces you to be more organized, aware, and unrelentingly patient while pursuing romance, but overall I feel the presence of children doesn't restrict your ability to have a relationship. Rather, it can create opportunities to enhance and expand your romantic life. Through your children's eyes, you see things about a potential mate you might otherwise miss (both good things and bad). You get to watch your child develop a relationship with another person beside yourself, you get to see that relationship grow and change, and through this process you will often see your kids in an entirely new light.

Your children, too, benefit in a number of ways: by having a mom who dates, they get a more realistic view of the world, which will better prepare them to enter that world when they are older. And by introducing them to new people with different backgrounds, ideas, and personalities, you are opening up their world in profound new ways.

> "*I think a single mom who dates brings variety to children. It teaches them about relationships, how to relate to others, and the beauty in diversity and in all people. It expands their social circle and makes them feel loved.*"
>
> —Lee 29, Seattle

Get out There (and Stop Denying Yourself)

The surest way to get your children used to the fact that you have a life of your own is to, well, actually *have* a life of your own. If you enjoy having cobwebs in your lingerie drawer, then by all means wait until your kids are in college to start dating. Otherwise, start educating them, and yourself, on how to merge motherhood and men.

chapter seven

The Mama

Sutra

WHEN IT COMES TO SEX,

SINGLE MOMS NEED

A WHOLE NEW REPERTOIRE

"Sex without love is an empty gesture.
But as empty gestures go, it is one of the best."
—Woody Allen

"You are a woman of many parts, Pussy."
—James Bond in *Goldfinger*

The title of this book has been the source of much consternation and concern for just about everyone involved—everyone, that is, except the single mothers for whom it was written. I was surprised to discover that even in this age of swinging suburbanites, trashy television shows, and prolific Internet porn, many people are downright prudish when it comes to seeing the words "sex" and "mom" in close proximity to one another. Toss in a little hand grenade like "single" in front of the sacred "mom," and you've upped the ante considerably.

The HBO series *Sex and the City* has been one of the biggest television hits of the last decade. Because the main characters were childless women—as opposed to single moms—everybody was pretty much okay with the almost constant on-screen sexcapades. But when one of the show's characters did, in fact, become a single mom, some people found themselves uncomfortable watching her almost futile attempts to remain a freewheeling, sexually liberated woman while at the same time caring for her newborn son.

I have to admit that often I was one of those people. I'm not sure if my discomfort came from the fact that the obstacles she confronted—cold-hearted bosses, skittish men, out-of-control hormones—reminded me a bit too much of my own life, or if perhaps I was just as programmed as the rest of society to see moms as non-sexual beings.

The irony of the situation is that single moms are ready, willing, and able to have sex and truly enjoy it. Single motherhood, rather than pushing us past our sexual prime, actually increases our awareness of our bodies, our need for intimacy, and our ability to multitask, which can definitely come in handy between the sheets. So rather than run away from this fact, let's embrace it and learn the ins and outs (so to speak) of sex and the single mom.

Why Are We So Good in Bed?

It's weird but true: there is a whole lot of porn created especially for guys who find sex-hungry moms a real turn-on. This could very well be the result of some Oedipal fantasy, but if you talk to a guy who's had the pleasure of dating a single mom, he will often comment on how great the sex was.

Why? Well, as we discussed in Chapter One, there are certain skills that you gain in parenting that can make you a better lover. As Dr. James Houran, who conducted a study of sexual attitudes and behavior for the online dating service www.true.com discovered, single mothers possess what he calls "parent-engendered" skills such as selflessness, flexibility, and stress management, all of which give us an edge over single women without children when it comes to a healthy sexual attitude—and appetite. In fact, single moms in the study tended to have strong libidos and an open mind when it comes to sex.

However, Dr. Pepper Schwartz notes that single moms also tend to vacillate between one extreme and the other when it comes to embracing, or repressing, sexual desire. "I think it's bimodal," she told me. "I think women tend to open up and get rid of some of their old prejudices about what's appropriate or not. They have to. Otherwise, they are going to go to the other extreme and not date or go out, and become a mother in capital letters—there is a danger in that, too."

Based upon the conversations I had with single moms while writing this book, I'd have to say that most of us moms are firmly planted in the sex-is a-good-thing camp. If there's one primary problem for these moms, it's finding the time—and an appropriate place—to have sex. This isn't a problem for married couples—they sleep together every night in the same old bed—yet oddly enough one constant refrain I hear from married friends is that they never have sex. Is this a case of you only want what you can't have, or is there something else going on?

"Let's face it," Dr. Schwartz says. "You can really love a movie, but if you see it ten times in a row, it's going to get old." She suggests that the unpredictability and time constraints inherent in a single mom's life can perhaps serve as an arousal mechanism. So it's a trade-off: you may not have a hubby at home to snuggle with every night, but your situation does open up the possibility of having some very hot, very unmarried sex once in a while. Combined with the fact that many single moms have been married or in long-term relationships before, which makes them generally more sexually experienced, and you have the makings of one very hot mama.

"I do think motherhood will make me a much better lover when I meet someone. I feel far more connected to what really matters in the world, more willing to take people as they are and not try to change them. I also feel I would be much better able to end something that wasn't working, and for something that was working, be very devoted to it. I feel parenting makes me more accepting and understanding of people's flaws, more tender—and that always helps love. On the physical side, if thirty hours of active labor and two years of breastfeeding don't make you uninhibited, I don't know what does."

—*Christine, 37, Boston*

Indeed, there are several advantages single moms possess when it comes to having healthy sex lives:

- The spinster stereotype is all but gone. Single moms are being portrayed as sexy and desirable instead of frumpy and unwanted. Television shows like *Desperate Housewives* and sexy, smart, and beautiful celebrity single moms like Meg Ryan and Katie Couric have made regular single moms feel like it's okay to celebrate—even show off—their sexy side.

- We've given birth. In general, this makes us less neurotic about all things sexual, including our bodies. As Dr. Carol Livoti, coauthor of the wonderful book *Vaginas: An Owner's Manual*, told me, "The whole labor experience demystifies and decreases the modesty around the vagina. I mean, think about delivery. Everyone's looking at your bottom."

- There's less at stake. This is not to mean that single moms take sex less seriously than women without children, but in general, there's just less tension. That's because we've already had our kids, and many of us have been married before, so we are more able to enjoy sex for its sake alone. There are fewer expectations attached to the act itself. We spend less time worrying, "Will he call tomorrow? Will we fall in love? Will we get married and have babies?" If we like someone a great deal there might be some of that going through our minds, but the fact that we've already been there allows us to some degree to relax more in bed and just let loose.

But sex as a single mom isn't all commitment-free flings and multiple orgasms. Some of the same advantages discussed above come with a flip side:

- The spinster stereotype is all but gone. In many circles, however, it's been replaced with the even more harmful single-mom-as-slut stereotype. Men may see you as an easy lay and treat you accordingly. This is insulting and can ultimately damage your self-esteem.

- We've given birth. This may make some moms less modest, but it also makes some less than pleased with their bodies. As Dr. Livoti points out, "Childbirth stretches your vagina way out of proportion. Before you had babies and you looked at a mirror, you would see the labia touching. Afterwards, you can see the opening to the vagina. This will improve over time, but then there's the ongoing problem with gravity."

- There's less at stake. The unbridled enthusiasm we bring into the bedroom can sometimes go too far. While it's important for any sexually active woman to protect herself against STDs, it is absolutely imperative for a single mother, since she needs to be there for her child today *and* tomorrow. This means you need to be certain to use condoms and to know your partner's sexual history. And lest we forget how we became moms in the first place, it's critical that we be vigilant about using birth control. All of which makes the prior mentioned spontaneity a little less, well, spontaneous.

"One man seemed genuinely interested in dating me. We went out a couple times. He then started pressuring me sexually, and when I didn't return his advances, he stopped calling me. I think maybe he thought since I had a kid I was easy."

—Dee, 25, Dallas

Sex Re-Education

As with most everything else, sex for single moms is different than it is for other women, in many different ways. As we discussed previously, our old ways of dating simply may not work now that we're moms. The same applies to the way we have sex. The equipment is the same, of course, albeit with a bit more wear and tear than before, and the basics haven't changed much. But the fact that you are now a mother and that you will eventually be having sex in your own home, where your children also happen to live, means you need to learn a few new tricks.

QUIET, PLEASE

Remember the good old days of having wild sex in just about any room in the house? No nook, cranny, or closet was off-limits to your libido. Now, however, you're more likely to get your kinks worked out in the chiropractor's office than you are rolling around on the kitchen floor with some sexy guy. And don't forget, your kids, neighbors, and even the family dog may be within earshot, so you also have to turn down the volume on your sexual sound effects. Anyway, if you have to be confined to a private place to have sex and you have to be quiet while you're doing it, you might be thinking you might as well just go to sleep instead. *Au contraire.* Don't give up on lovemaking just because of these limitations. Instead, see it as an opportunity. For instance, if your bedroom is really the only "safe" room in the house to have sex (read: the only room that has a door with a lock on it), you now have an incentive to make it an inviting, sensual, and intimate place—which means no Goldfish crackers in the bed or piles of pop-up books all over the floor. Consider candles, nice sheets, and shades that cover all of your windows. You can add a small CD player or stereo or one of those relaxing little indoor fountains to provide a bit of soundproofing. Once you've soundproofed your space, you'll need to soundproof yourself, which means keeping those moans, meows, or whatever your usual noises are under wraps. Quiet doesn't have to mean boring, however. In fact, the intensity and focus required in order to be quiet during sex can be something of a turn-on. It forces you to be even more intimate with your partner and to truly feel what's going on with your two bodies. And whispers, murmers, and sighs are all sensual, erotic ways to fuel arousal without rousing the kids sleeping down the hall.

WORK IT, BABY

Could you ever have imagined, in your preparenthood days, that you'd one day have to worry about whether or not your vagina was in shape? Thighs, butt, tummy, sure, but not the love canal—that was always pretty much okay. Then you pushed something out of it that was roughly the size of a watermelon, and your vagina hasn't ever let you forget it. Even if you had a C-section, if you breast-fed your baby, your formerly firm and shapely breasts may now be hanging a little loose. Basically, childbirth can wreak havoc with the very parts of our anatomy where men like to spend the most time. It's not fair, but your breasts and vagina may never be the same as they once were. However, by spending a few minutes a day whipping 'em into shape, you'll feel better about your body when you're in the buff. For strengthening your vagina, Kegel exercises are best, and best of all, you can do them without having to go anywhere. Kegel exercises tone up the muscles around the vagina and urethra and improve blood flow to those areas. Many women have found that by doing Kegels on a consistent basis, they are able to get more pleasure during intercourse. "They do work," Dr. Carol Livoti told me, "and there are even physical therapists who specialize in vaginal strengthening." A more radical option is vaginoplasty, a surgical procedure that makes the vagina tighter by removing excess vaginal lining and tightening the surrounding soft tissues. Dr. Livoti cautions, however, that there are risks. "Well, look at Michael Jackson's nose. There are always risks with plastic surgery." So if you ever want to be friends with your vagina again, you should start doing Kegels now—it's easy. Simply identify the muscles you use to stop the flow of urine when you pee. Obviously, to properly locate these muscles the first time, you'll need to do so while urinating. Now, isolate and tighten those muscles *without* tightening your abdominal or buttocks muscles for four seconds and then release for four seconds. Repeat ten to fifteen times. Try to do four sets a day to start. To help perk up droopy breasts, easy exercises such as chest flies using five-pound weights or even push-ups will help firm your chest, back, arms, and abdominal muscles, all of which contribute to making your breasts appear more uplifted. Here again, there is a surgical option: the breast lift is a procedure designed to raise and reshape sagging breasts. Sometimes breast implants are inserted while the breasts are lifted. But the best, cheapest, and fastest lift of all is to simply maintain good posture. Time, gravity, and childbearing are all working against your breasts; the least you can do is a little work on their behalf and stand up straight.

OPEN YOUR MIND (AND YOUR LEGS)

Even if your sex life with your former partner was satisfying, you now have the opportunity to take things to another level. You have a clean slate, if you will, and are free to act on fantasies and desires you may have been too embarrassed to share with your child's father. However, some women feel that, because they are moms, doing so is shameful or, at the very least, not very parentlike. On the contrary, though, a healthy approach to sexual desire can only help you be better prepared when your children start developing their own sexual personalities. Anyone who has ever had a sexually repressed parent who made their kids feel that sex is dirty and to be avoided at all costs knows the negative effects it can have on their adult lives and relationships. If this is an issue you struggle with, get some good books, go to some seminars, spend more time masturbating, study the *Kama Sutra*, watch a porn movie—do whatever it takes to get in tune with your innate sexuality. Well, do whatever it takes within reason, because, after all, you do have children, and the only thing more damaging than creating shame around sex is to make them feel it's okay to be sexually irresponsible. The point is that you are now free to take advantage of the sexual freedoms that come with being a single mom—so go ahead, take a walk on the wild side.

WRITE YOUR OWN MAMA SUTRA

Tired of reading about sexual positions that assume you once had a career as a contortionist? Then why not invent some bedroom positions of your own, based upon things you already know you can do? I'm talking about moves that only a mother could know, such as the piggy back ride. The tickle attack (there are sensitive spots beside armpits). The laundry lift (if you guessed this involves lots of bending over, you're right, but you'll enjoy it a lot more than the daily load you're used to). Or what about the diaper change? Lay on your back, lift your bottom, and slide off your panties. Now if your partner starts to reach for the baby powder, you may be taking it a bit too far, but you get the idea.

FAST-FOOD SEX

Let me say right off the bat, I'm not going to advocate you start dropping your drawers for every dude that catches your eye. But sometimes, just once in a while, it can be very good to be very bad. Just like when you break your vow to not stop at that greasy drive-through joint, the one you pass every day on your way to work, sometimes you just have to say "screw it" and go get yourself some. And afterwards, you'll be glad you did because it was so yummy and, hell, you deserved it! Well, fast-food sex is kind of like that. Where can you get it? Like its high-cholesterol counterpart, it's available on practically every street corner. You need to be selective, of course, but let's face it, you're in a hurry. You could be at a party or in line at the grocery store. Maybe you're out of town on business. It doesn't really matter where you are: You've been a good girl, you've been careful, but right now you're really hungry and you just want to feel full. So you go for it. You don't stand around studying the menu. You order, you get your fill, and you get the heck out of there. Afterwards, you vow to never eat there again, because, really, it's not very healthy. That is, until the next time.

How to Think Like a Guy
(If You Dare)

Your sexual re-education requires not only getting in touch with your own wants and needs but also learning what makes a man happy. Before you get into a guy's pants, you need to climb inside his head. This can be a scary place to visit, I know, but if you can get grip on how he thinks before you seduce him, you won't be thrown for a loop when he says and does the damnedest things. And trust me, he will.

Allow me to share some of the surprising facts about guys that I've learned from my own experiences and from talking to other sexually active single moms.

HE'S A DICK — AND THEN SOME

Just as men can sometimes objectify women, we have been known to see guys as just a means to an end, the end being a great orgasm. There's nothing wrong with that in the right context (see "Fast-Food Sex," left), but if you really want to get the most out of the limited amount of time you spend with men, you need to understand that there's a lot more to them than a really nice hard-on. Given that many guys still go to great lengths to cover up their feelings, this can be difficult to believe. But it's true. And if he's chosen you, a single mom, to spend time with, chances are there's a lot more to him than meets the eye. So give him the benefit of the doubt and get to know him a little bit outside of the bedroom, too.

HE'S AFRAID OF THE KIDS

More to the point, he's scared to death of the children catching you two in bed. The presence of kids in the house while you're making love can wilt his awesome erection faster than you can say "It's okay, I talked to my daughter about the birds and bees." So don't be cavalier about the issue. Explain to him you understand why he's nervous—you are, too—and if he's still uncomfortable, offer to have sex somewhere else for a while. In the meantime, you may want to reread "Quiet, Please," above.

YOUR STRETCH MARKS DON'T BOTHER HIM

I know they bother *you*, but many men are actually in awe of our ability to carry and deliver a child, and the subsequent scars from your journey to motherhood generate feelings and emotions even they cannot completely understand. However, if he's one of those shallow idiots who thinks stretch marks or a postpartum pooch are gross, and he lets you know it, feel free to tell him how you feel about that growing bald spot at the back of his head—then show him the door.

HE APPRECIATES SEX WITH YOU MORE BECAUSE IT'S HARDER TO COME BY

Single women without children have the advantage of being available for sex anytime, anyplace. This, however, can be a disadvantage, as it can cause the initial attraction to wear off that much faster and her constant availability can even bore some guys. We don't have that problem, because we're hardly ever available to hop in the sack. When we do manage to squeeze it in, so to speak, he's very grateful to get some—and so are you.

"I used to be very uptight about stretch marks, but now I see them as medals and wear them proudly, just as a soldier would wear a purple heart. Pregnancy is hard work, as is labor, delivery, and

raising a child. Sure it changes your body but look at what a beautiful prize you get in the end."

—Susan, 34, Kentucky

"I am not thrilled with my body after nursing and giving birth to two children. I have the saggy breasts, the extra baby fat around my tummy, and stretch marks covering half my body, but I am also more in tune with my body. I am more aware of my body and know how to ask for pleasure."

—Lee, 29, Seattle

YOUR STATUS AS A MOTHER TURNS HIM ON— AND SCARES THE CRAP OUT OF HIM

He knows you can get pregnant, since you already have, so he is ultraparanoid about conception. So go ahead, hand him a box of condoms.

MEN, SEX, AND MOTHERS

Once when I was having problems with an old boyfriend, he blurted out that maybe his "Madonna-whore complex" was the source of all his neuroses. I paused for a minute and replied that just because he thinks Madonna is a whore, what's that got to do with us? He looked at me with something akin to pity, patted me on the back, and simply said, "Look it up, sweetheart." So I did. And suddenly, a whole bunch of things about him and other men that had passed through my life became much clearer. It seems that men have been hung up about sex and their mothers forever. The following are the two major hang-ups you'll encounter.

The Madonna-whore complex: I spoke to a bunch of single moms who told me their marriages ended after their husbands started screwing around—and this often happened not long after their kids came along. Why this tendency to mess around on Mommy? Psychologists believe it's related to how some men view women as one of two distinct personas, either as a saint or a sinner, a mother or a whore. She can be one or the other, but never both. If a man had a particularly intense, unusually close relationship with his mom (a "smother" rather than a "mother"), he may be more susceptible to the Madonna-whore complex. Once you become a mom, you remind him of his own mother, and to have sex with you on some level feels incestuous. Now, the good news is that any new men in our lives will not be the biological father of our children, and the complex is usually associated with married men who can no longer feel sexual toward the mother of their own children. But still, there are men who associate mothers of any kind with sainthood, and if you slink into the bedroom in garters and a bustier, he will probably freak out. Men who have this complex are to be avoided, because you're a mother and nothing is going to change that.

The Oedipus complex: Sigmund Freud famously developed the notion of the Oedipus complex. According to this theory, children at a very young age have an unconscious desire for sexual intercourse with their parent of the opposite sex. This is especially prevalent between boys and their mothers. (The Oedipus complex is named after the mythical Oedipus, who unwittingly killed his father and married his mother.) During infancy, the theory goes, a boy becomes attached to his mother, a daughter to her father. Freud believed that the resolution of this attachment is necessary for a normal sexual life. Some experts believe that an unresolved Oedipus complex can be an important factor in the subsequent creation of the Madonna-whore complex, since a man's mother was his first love object. I believe if you are involved with a guy like this, you should kick him off your couch and tell him to park his rear on a shrink's instead. There's enough craziness in your life as it is.

Pillow Talk: What Men Wish We Wouldn't Do in Bed

If you want to see the same guy naked more than once, pay attention to these simple rules.

SKIP THE BEDTIME STORIES

What is it about lying prone on a mattress next to someone that makes us have diarrhea of the mouth? Things we would never dream of telling a guy in any other setting spill forth like someone's just shot us up with truth serum. I know it's tempting to want to fill the awkward, quiet space that fills the room following sex, especially with someone you don't know well. However, after sex most men want to do one of three things: sleep, get another erection, or go to the bathroom. You'll notice that "talking about your innermost feelings" isn't anywhere on that list. I know this is a huge generalization, and some guys are more than happy to have a postcoital chat. If he's a talker, feel free to engage with him, but pay very close attention to what you're saying, because, believe me, he is. This is not the time to share your most intimate feelings, dreams, hopes, fears, and needs, at least until you've been together a long, long time. Keep your mouth shut, and if you can't, then talk about safe subjects such as baseball and the weather.

DON'T CONFUSE SEX WITH LOVE

An entire book could be written about how women often equate sex with commitment and caring, and how this drives men insane. It's not that they don't care or aren't interested in commitment—some are, some aren't—but when these topics are brought up just before, during, or after sex, they take on a whole new flavor—one that men don't find very tasty. If they're not sure how they feel about you, for example, you risk making them feel obligated to you because you're having sex. Maybe he was headed in that direction already, but now he's just scared. Or, if he wasn't planning on heading toward love and commitment with you, the subject coming up in such an intimate context could make him feel guilty. And I don't think I need to repeat how guys feel about guilt. Certainly, if you really like someone, you'll want to get a sense of where he's at. That's fine, but do it at another time and place to avoid making him even more uncomfortable than he no doubt already is.

PICK UP YOUR TOYS

It's totally unfair, but while guys can get away with being porn-addicted, Hooters-loving horndogs, we women still need to exhibit some level of decorum, in their convoluted minds, at least. So while he may love the fact that you tie him to the bed posts or don fishnets and high heels, because you are a mother, he expects the evidence of your sexcapades to remain safely hidden and that any discussion of what you do together remain your little secret. In other words, pick up the handcuffs and put them away before your kids find them and they start playing cops and robbers, because otherwise your man will see you as irresponsible. That's just his way of projecting his shame and embarrassment onto you, but hey, there it is.

> "I've always had a low opinion about my body but these days, I feel like a goddess most of the time—having a child has made me feel better about myself."
>
> —Jasmine, 43, Toronto

Sex and the Single Mom: Good and Getting Better

As single moms become more empowered in other aspects of their lives, including their careers, their parenting skills, and their ability to care for themselves, sexual empowerment will naturally follow. Some people may still be a bit queasy about single mothers living sexually active lives, but that's really not your problem. You deserve a healthy, pleasurable sex life just as much as the next woman, and if you're open, aware, and enthusiastic, trust me, you're gonna get it.

chapter eight

Tie Me Up, Tie Me Down?

WHY DO WE ASSUME MARRIAGE

WILL MAKE MOTHERHOOD EASIER?

*"Any intelligent woman who reads
the marriage contract, and then goes into it,
deserves all the consequences."*
—Isadora Duncan

*"One of the oddest features of western
Christianized culture is its ready acceptance of
the myth of the stable family and the happy marriage.
We have been taught to accept the myth not as
an heroic ideal, something good, brave, and
nearly impossible to fulfill, but as the very fibre of
normal life. Given most families and most marriages,
the belief seems admirable but foolhardy."*
—Jonathan Raban, British author and critic

In a stunning shift of attitudes, single moms, in some circles, have become the object of envy instead of pity. I can't tell you how many married women with children have said to me, "Well, at least you don't have to take care of a husband *and* kids." And even some men have told me they think I have the best of both worlds—a family of my own *and* my freedom. So after decades of being teased, scorned, feared, and discriminated against by those who are married, we are finally in position to feel, if not quite superior, at least pretty damn good about our single status. So why don't we?

Well, some of us do and some of us don't. A strong current of ambivalence and contradiction was apparent in my interviews with single moms and relationship experts. On the one hand, we're happy to no longer be in a dysfunctional marriage or partnership. On the other hand, there are times when we'd give anything to be married or in a committed long-term relationship again. One day a study concludes a two-parent household is best for children; the next day another study seems to indicate children raised in single-parent households are doing just fine. This schizophrenia comes with the territory of single motherhood, and to some extent, we have to go on this roller coaster ride and try to enjoy it. But for some single moms, the quest for an altar-worthy guy takes precedence over just about everything else, including, sometimes, the kids. This is not a good way to go through life. You need a reality check, and I'm here to give it to you.

Here I outline the pros and cons of having a spouse or partner while you are raising your children. And while the jury is still out on whether or not children need both parents at home to succeed, no one can refute that the divorce rate in this country remains high: 40 to 50 percent of all first marriages are projected to end in divorce, and for second and third marriages, the rate of divorce is even higher.

After reading this chapter you may still be bouncing back and forth between your twin desires to be single and to be married, but at least you'll be looking at marriage with open eyes instead of through decades-old rose-colored glasses.

First Comes Love,
Then Comes Marriage . . .

Q. How is a marriage like our mother's womb?

A. The minute we're out of it, all we want to do is get back in.

There is nothing wrong with you for wanting a husband. Your entire life you have been conditioned to believe that they're something you need to survive, right up there with food, water, and oxygen. If you combine this societal brainwashing with having a mom and dad who were married for a gazillion years, you're going to have a really hard time letting go of your desire for a two-carat diamond on your left hand and a date for Valentine's Day every year for the rest of your life.

But let's face facts: You're reading this book because you're a single mom, which means you have already broken the traditional marriage mold and there's no going back. You can't send your kids back from whence they came and start over with a stable two-parent family. That may make you sad, but please realize that you are not alone. Households in America headed by a single parent number in the tens of millions, and those numbers are heading up. So take comfort in the fact that you are a lot closer to the norm than you might think. As Stephanie Coontz, author of *Marriage, A History: From Obedience to Intimacy, or How Love Conquered Marriage*, writes in the *Washington Post*, "In the United States and Britain, divorce rates fell slightly during the 1990s, but the incidence of cohabitation and unmarried child-raising continues to rise, as does the percentage of singles in the population. Both trends reduce the social significance of marriage in the economy and culture." Coontz goes on to toss out a startling statistic to support her claim that marriage is losing ground as the dominant lifestyle choice for parents: "Today, 40 percent of cohabiting couples in the United States have children in the household, almost as high a proportion as the 45 percent of married couples who have kids, according to the 2000 Census." She goes on to say that "marriage as a public institution exerts less power over people's lives now that the majority of Americans spend half their adult lives outside marriage and almost half of all kids spend part of their childhood in a household that does not include their two married biological parents."

> *"I'm not sure what the future holds for me, but I can tell you this much: If no suitable man comes along for me and my daughter, I am very much content being single."*
>
> —Dee, 25, Dallas

So remember, there is nothing at all wrong with you. I can't say this enough, so I'll say it again: *There is nothing wrong with not being married.* On the contrary, there is a lot that's *right* with you, such as:

- You are not settling. Even if you did lower your standards for a while, you had the guts to get out of a bad relationship. Or, if you were the one who was left, you've shown you have *cojones* to rebuild your life without a partner.

- You are putting parenting first. Many of the single moms interviewed for this book cited their desire for a happy, stable household as their primary reason for leaving a marriage or resisting the temptation to jump into another one too soon. This irony is completely lost on proponents of marriage as a fix for society's ills, but single moms certainly get it.

- You are living in the real world. Most single moms agree that a good marriage or long-term committed partnership is a worthy goal to aspire to. They aren't antimarriage or anti-relationship by any means. However, many of the moms I've talked to simply don't see the point in establishing a partnership unless the end result is a better, more fulfilling family life for themselves and their kids than the one they have now. Not just a little bit better, but a *lot* better. And most single moms have very realistic expectations about the work involved in making a partnership succeed.

- You are not wasting your hard-won freedom. Finding a hubby is no longer first on your list of priorities. Important life goals such as going back to school, becoming more involved with your kids' education, or taking that trip to Europe you've dreamed of forever are the activities you're investing your energy in now. Rather than wasting your dateless nights by throwing yourself a pity party, you realize that if you were married, you might have to sacrifice some of your personal goals to focus on the partnership and your life together as a family.

"I have never been married, so I cannot say with the utmost confidence that I prefer to be single, but I do enjoy life as a single parent.

I hear horror stories of other people's relationships, and I do not miss all the work involved."

—Lee, 29, Seattle

The Grass Is Always Greener— Because It's Really Astroturf

The view from your sometimes lonely little perch in single mom land can be bleak at times, which makes married life look awfully good by comparison. You imagine that with a husband, you would have a companion, a helper, a friend, and a lover. And there are some days that single motherhood is so unbelievably hard you'd give just about anything to have a partner. "I think it depends on the age of the mom," says Dr. Pepper Schwartz. "I think the ones with younger children are really busy, and they'd love a partner to handle things with. It's tough."

FEELING TRASHED

For me, the toughest moment to be without a husband was always garbage night. I didn't find taking out the trash physically difficult, but rather emotionally grueling. On the dreaded night I'd wheel my big, overflowing can to the curb while the kids were in the house screaming and running around like wild animals. The overstuffed container would wobble and, inevitably, a bunch of garbage would spill out onto the driveway. Sometimes, I was so exhausted I just left the stuff there and picked it up the next morning.

Eventually, I'd get the can to the curb and look across the street. And there they'd be, my neighbors' helpful husbands taking out the trash while their wives were inside the house doing wifey things. These guys would wave at me and offer a sad little smile. I would feel like a fool and a total loser, standing there in my sweats and T-shirt, with my equally unkempt garbage can by my side.

I allowed this stupid household chore to beat me down emotionally for quite some time, that is, until I had an extended stay with some friends of mine, a married couple. Every night the trash can would sit near the back door, waiting to be emptied into the big can outside. And every night my friend would ask her husband—gently at first—to please take it out. Please. Can you take out the trash, *please*? Eventually her polite request would turn into a full-fledged roar, and yet, sometimes when I got up the next morning, the wastebasket was still sitting there, smelly and defiant.

After that, I didn't feel as bad taking out my own garbage. I figured chances were pretty good that at married people's homes there were at least some threats or screams involved in getting the damn can ten yards down the driveway on Tuesday nights. Something I didn't envy—not one bit.

These days I actually feel a bit of pride when I wheel the rickety can to the curb. And if a little bit of garbage spills out of the top, I bend over, pick it up, and stuff it back in. Then I wave at my neighbor, smile a sympathetic little smile, and go back inside to play with my kids.

Sure, some things *would* be easier if we had husbands, but married life would not be the perfect vision that it sometimes looks like from afar. Some of these illusions are the product of our own active imaginations and from having spent way too much time watching *Leave It to Beaver* reruns. But much of this rosy picture is painted *for* us. After all, lots of people have a vested interest in making you believe married couples have better lives and raise better kids. Many of these people are men in positions of power who are determined to prevent a matriarchal society from taking hold in this country, a topic I'll discuss more in the final chapter of this book. Mostly, though, the insecure, close-minded folks who are stuck in miserable marriages are the loudest proponents of the institution. Misery loves company, after all.

Even many of those with happy marriages are dead set on putting an end to your single status. They will set you up with any loser they can find because your freedom as a single woman threatens them and, they believe, their marriage. Even though you're about as likely to sleep with your eighty-year-old doorman as your best friend's husband, your friend might, on some subconscious level, be uneasy with you being all footloose and fancy-free around her man.

The incredibly annoying thing about this kind of paranoia is that it assumes the worst about you, and it completely ignores the reality of your life. You have so little time and energy because of the demands of single parenting that seducing the neighbor is about the last thing on your mind. But none of that matters, because until you are "one of them"—that is, married—you are one of *them*, a woman without a husband. People who see the world in these black-and-white terms are stuck in a time warp that's positively frightening. Deep down, you know this, but still you sometimes wonder if they may be right. Sometimes you wonder why you can't have what they have . . .

Which is *what* exactly? Here are some of some of the assumed benefits of being married:

- A second income. A husband means you'll have some help paying the bills. Then again, some husbands choose to stay home, or they lose their jobs, or they mismanage the family finances.

- More help at home. A second pair of hands around the house would be really nice, wouldn't it? But many married women will tell you that their husband's hands are most often occupied holding the TV remote or a golf club or the computer mouse. This isn't always the case, but there is no shortage of polls that indicate married mothers with full-time jobs still feel they do the majority of the housework.

- Someone to help raise the kids. Is this really what you want? Be careful what you wish for in this case, and be very clear with yourself what you mean. Many single moms I heard from don't want a partner to tell them how to parent. Some mothers, especially those with young boys, felt that having a male influence on their children would be an asset, but this is different from wanting someone to take over disciplining your kids and serving as the primary caregiver.

- Regular sex and affection. Marriage isn't Viagra. It can't guarantee you'll be having hot sex seven nights a week, nor does it even necessarily mean you'll be cuddling and giving each other long, luxurious back rubs. Basically, it means there's a guy around a lot more often, should the time, energy, and interest arise to do those things. But you could say the same thing about having a lover or boyfriend. In short, having a husband doesn't assure your sexual and romantic needs will always be met.

> *"Part of me yearns for a real relationship, but the other part tells me that if I fall head over heels, all the other things I've been working for in my life could suffer. Then what? What would I do if the relationship failed? Taking that plunge is a very touchy subject. Sometimes love or lust isn't worth it."*
>
> —*Maggie, 42, Denver*

All Bets Are Off

At one time or another, every parent frustrated with a difficult child has heard that the child is simply going through a phase, but single mothers go through phases as well. Neediness, independence, ambivalence, and resignation are all phases that we experience as we move in and out of relationships, or convince ourselves that we must be married in order to be happy, then change our minds about it once again.

The desire for a life partner is natural one, but so is a mother's desire to spend her remaining years focused on motherhood first, with career or personal goals second and men coming in a distant third. As Stephanie Coontz aptly puts it, "In today's climate of choice, many people's choices do not involve marriage. We must recognize that there are healthy as well as unhealthy ways to be single or to be divorced, just as there are healthy and unhealthy ways to be married. We cannot afford to construct our social policies, our advice to our own children and even our own emotional expectations around the illusion that all commitments, sexual activities and caregiving will take place in a traditional marriage."

Most importantly, you need to remember you are already in the most important relationship of your life, the one between you and your child. As Dr. Pepper Schwartz tells me, "I think the advantage that single moms have is that they have their kids. They are a great source of company and emotional engagement and another entrée into the world. I think as a single person without kids, you could start to feel unloved if you haven't met a guy in a long time. But if you have children who you have a good relationship with, you have love in your life. You're not that needy. You may want a guy, but you really do have love in your life and even better, you have a place to express it."

And who knows? Maybe someday you can even get your kid to take out the garbage without even having to ask. Maybe.

chapter nine

The Other "F" Words

FRIENDS, FILMS, AND FARAWAY PLACES—

ROMANTIC SUBSTITUTES THAT REALLY WORK

"The best time to make friends is before you need them."
—Ethel Barrymore

*"Lots of people want to ride with you
in the limo, but what you want is someone who will take
the bus with you when the limo breaks down."*
—Oprah Winfrey

When Hillary Clinton coined the phrase "It takes a village," she seemed to be speaking directly to us. After all, who needs an extended support network more than single moms? In addition to a supportive family, your village must include a great video store, a stable of like-minded friends of both sexes, and the ability to travel lightly if you are to create a fulfilling life on your own.

For some single mothers, the very idea that they can have a fun and productive life in between boyfriends is a challenging concept. The assumption is that if you're not doing something with somebody else, it's not worth doing. In this chapter, you'll learn why it's not so bad to be without a romantic partner, and how, with your hectic life, in many cases it's a blessing.

Quit Yer Bitchin'

Admit it: when you're in a committed relationship, you can get frustrated at times because you have neither the freedom nor the time you once did. Between the kids and the guy, there are not enough hours in the day for you, let alone your friends—and you can forget about hobbies. Perhaps you keep a little list of all the things you'd do if you only had the time: learn to speak French, backpack in Costa Rica, homeschool the kids, train for a marathon, and write the great American novel. Your list of goals and dreams is long, and you might assume it will take ages to accomplish any of it.

And then you and your partner split. You're still going to be busy with parenting and work, but guess what? A big gaping hole just opened up in your schedule. This is great news! You can get out your list and start doing all those things you've always wanted to.

But do you? Probably not. Instead you focus on finding another guy, or you obsess about the breakup or slip into a funk where you don't want to do a damn thing. That's to be expected— for a short time. But realize that at some point, maybe even sooner than you expect, you'll probably be in a relationship again, which will again cut into your precious time and energy. So stop complaining about where you're at today and instead make the most of it. Take those classes. Ring up that long-lost friend. Start going to your kids' baseball games again or hit the gym.

This advice is not meant to convince you simply to fill up your time so that you miss having a man less. Instead, it is meant to help you build a long-lasting, reliable foundation for your entire life. Because as we all know, relationships begin and end all the time. When the next one is over, you'll want to feel as strong and as supported as possible. You'll want to be able to jump back into the things you love with little to no ramp-up time.

So pull out your to-do list, dig up your address book, unearth your suitcase—and let's build you a village.

What Are Friends For?

In my late teens and early twenties, I noticed that my girlfriends and I had developed a really bad habit: we talked on a fairly regular basis, but we never called each other to actually *do* something together unless we were unattached. The minute we had a new boyfriend we'd disappear off the face of the earth, only to reemerge after it was all over, to lick our wounds, look for sympathy, and find someone to buy us several drinks.

Being flaky about friendships like this might be okay in your youth. But once you are a single parent, you need true friends that you can always count on. Friends who love you unconditionally are precious assets, not to be used or abused, because, trust me, you are going to need them, and at some point they are going to need you, especially if they too are single parents.

That said, you'll want to make sure the people you currently call your friends are, in fact, good for you. It takes a special kind of man or woman to understand your crazy life and to support you through the many ups and downs of child rearing alone. Perhaps this is why there are so many single mom social and support groups—it takes one to know one. However, I have married friends, single childless friends, single parent friends, gay friends, and straight friends. They are all very different, yet they share one critical character trait: they do not judge me. They accept my status as a single mom as a part of who I am. When I show up at their parties without a date, they don't razz me, and they don't set me up on blind dates with men they know I won't like. These are the kinds of friends you need. Without them, it's easy to feel lost, isolated, or downright weird.

If you are divorced, you may have been dismayed to discover that some of your married friends disappeared into the woodwork when you became a single parent. Dinner party invites were fewer and far between, and you'd hear about your married friends doing something together as a group—without you. As discussed in the previous chapter, some married people just feel uncomfortable around single moms. That's a drag, but when it's your friends that are giving you the cold shoulder, it can be heartbreaking.

See it as a sign that it's time for you to move on and make some new friends. This can be difficult, but it's not impossible. I've found that life just seems to bring us the right people at the right time, although I have to admit that sometimes I wish life would speed things up a bit. But good friends, like a good guy, are definitely worth the wait.

MEGAN THE MIGHTY

I'd see her come and go from the condo across from mine, all dark hair, funky hats, and a slow, moody saunter. And always, following just a few feet behind, was a young boy, around nine, with piles of long brown curls and smooth ivory skin. We lived across from each other for months but never spoke. She'd see me with my boys, splashing in the community hot tub, or in the morning as I was rushing off to work.

I finally got the courage to talk to her one day when she was unloading a piece of furniture from her beat-up old truck. "Need some help?" I asked. "No, it's okay, I got it." She obviously didn't—the big table threatened to tumble out right on top of her—and that's when I knew she must be a single mom. Her stubbornly self-sufficient attitude was a dead giveaway. I came over and helped her anyway, and a great friendship was born.

During the months we were neighbors, I learned that Megan was a single mom by choice. When her boyfriend found out she was pregnant, he wanted none of it and that was that. Megan had received a number of marriage proposals, including one from the father of her child after he decided he could "put up with a kid," but she turned them all down. She just couldn't see any reason to get married, and now that she was a mom, she felt even more strongly about it. Her independence intrigued me and, ultimately, inspired me not to settle for just any guy or to get married simply for marriage's sake.

Over the next several months, whenever I needed help or just someone to talk to, she was always there. She wasn't someone I'd known for years, and in fact I knew very little about her, but her actions told me all I needed to know. I trusted her.

Not long after we started hanging out, I had to move closer to work. We were both bummed; we kept saying, why didn't we meet sooner? What stopped us from introducing ourselves? Pride, perhaps, with a little fear thrown in. We'd both been hurt, and we'd both spent too much time alone. Letting people in isn't always easy for single moms. Once you do, make sure the person who is walking into your life is someone you respect and the kind of friend who will be there for you through good times and bad. In other words, someone just like you.

Social Studies

Have you ever felt like good friends are harder to find than a good guy? Especially as we get older, it seems everyone already has a firmly established group or "tribe." The search for friends is also compounded by fatigue, financial constraints, and, often, rusty social skills. Before we were parents, expanding our social lives was as easy as stepping out the front door. We could go anywhere, and do anything we wanted. We made friends easily, and it seemed like someone was always up for going out and doing something. Childbirth changed all of that. Suddenly you went from having a life to being responsible for someone else's. You spent a great deal of time in semi-isolation as you recovered from birth, either on maternity leave or by quitting work altogether to stay at home with your child. You're not exactly cut off from the world, but you're not out meeting and greeting either. Your childless friends are all out enjoying life, while you're at home having a nervous break-down from lack of sleep.

> *"I had never been alone before. I had always been with a steady boyfriend. So when I was single and a mom, I felt like no one would want me. The other college girls were partying, buying sexy clothes, going clubbing. I was just trying to hide the stretch marks and get in bed by nine o'clock every night!"*
>
> —*Julie, 21, Boston*

Unfortunately, the lack of social interaction that often follows childbirth can turn some previously outgoing single moms into veritable hermits. Even if you're not one of those, you may find that while you've been busy raising kids, a lot of your friends have moved on. So how do you get back in the swing of things and start meeting people to populate your village? First, make sure you really *want* a more active social life. After all, there's nothing wrong with spending lots of time alone or focusing mainly on your children as long as you're happy. If you force yourself to get out more and interact with others when you'd really rather be home doing the *New York Times* crossword puzzle or painting the bathroom, that'll be written all over your face and people will probably steer clear of you. Then you'll feel like a social misfit and vow to never venture out of your cave again.

However, for those who feel like it's time to make some new acquaintances, here are some tips on how get started. (By the way, new friends can be a great source of dates. You're "new" on the market as far as their social circle goes, and many are more than happy to introduce you around.)

> *"Single moms are less materialistic and lower maintenance. This can attract some very interesting people."*
>
> —Jasmine, 43, Toronto

MIX IT UP

Previously we talked about the benefits of dating "against type," of breaking out of your tired routine of dating the same sorts of guys over and over. The same advice applies to making new friends. If you've been in a rut lately, hanging out only with other moms or, conversely, only with childless women, you're missing out on a whole lot of interesting folks. Personally, I enjoy having friends much younger than myself and friends from different cultural backgrounds—they make my life more interesting just by knowing them. I also cherish my friendships with men. I think single moms are particularly prone to cutting themselves off from men, especially if they've had horrible romantic experiences in the past. But guy friends are a great way to surround yourself with male energy, and what's more, they tend to hang out with other guys, which means you've just increased your odds of meeting a man who's a known quantity. So when you think about reinventing your social set, resist the urge to fill your address book with more of the same old, same old and put yourself in places where you're likely to meet a variety of active, outgoing people.

FIND A CONTEXT

In our quest for love, many of us aspire to meeting our soul mate by chance and making beautiful music together for the rest of our lives. Although this does happen on occasion, people more often find their match in a setting where they find they have something in common. This is also true for lasting friendships; you're more likely to meet high-quality and highly compatible people in classes, seminars, nature clubs, or political or parenting groups that interest you. And don't forget the Internet—services like Friendster and myspace.com; these and others are popular ways to meet new people without having to leave the house.

CUT YOUR LOSSES

No doubt dozens of friends and acquaintances will pass through your life over the years. Now that you're a single mom, however, you need to have the backbone to give the heave-ho to any friend who is draining your energy or just making your already difficult life even harder. You know, people who complain all the time or only call you when they need a shoulder to cry on, or worse, are always asking to borrow money or your car. This is tough to do if you're already feeling lonely and like you need all the friends you can get, but in the long run, an unhealthy friendship is just like a dysfunctional romance: it has no place in your life whatsoever. You have a great deal to offer, so never sell yourself short.

The Next Best Things

There's no denying it: friends are one thing, but they're not the same as having a loving partner to share your life with. When you're without a significant other, life can feel lonely even when you're busy and surrounded by other people all the time. How do you alleviate the longing for a partner that you'll inevitably experience when you've been single for a while?

My advice is to embrace and experience it. Suppressing your romantic, sentimental side isn't healthy and can make it that much harder to open up again once you do meet someone who gets your heart pounding.

This is where another "F" word, *films*, can be particularly cathartic. By now you've probably picked up on the fact that I'm a big movie aficionado, so I'm biased on this one. But when I'm in between relationships, I find that certain films can make me feel better—that is, after they've made me feel worse. Because as any woman who's ever watched a chick flick or anything with Bogey and Bacall in it can tell you, movies are strategically designed to pull at your heartstrings. They do this by playing into our childhood fantasies of the knight in shining armor and, of course, The Happy Ending. In movies, love conquers all. We know this isn't true in real life but aren't our lives filled with enough reality? Sometimes you need a celluloid escape.

A SELECTED FILM-MOM-GRAPHY

I've pared down my unbelievably long list of favorite films to thirty movies that are particularly suited for the single mom, or just plain good films, perfect for those times when you need a good cry or a lot of laughs:

An Unmarried Woman	*This Boy's Life*
Enchanted April	*Baby Boom*
Kramer vs. Kramer	*Waiting to Exhale*
The War of the Roses	*Look Who's Talking*
School of Rock	*The Others*
Erin Brockovich	*The Way We Were*
Norma Rae	*Freaky Friday*
Parenthood	*You Can Count on Me*
Mommie Dearest	*Out of Africa*
Anywhere but Here	*The Hours*
Mermaids	*As Good As It Gets*

Get Outta Here

You've overdosed on flicks, your friends are screening their calls, and even the Internet is boring you to death. You feel restless and you fear that if you don't do something—quick—you're going to call up your old boyfriend or try something really desperate, like speed dating. Don't go there—instead, go to your closet and pull out your suitcase. Not the mondo one you use for long trips, but something light, squishy, and colorful—a weekend vacation bag.

Next, go to the phone and start dialing. Start with your regular sitter and work your way down the list, calling friends, family, neighbors—anyone you trust to watch the kids for forty-eight hours. You're going on a road trip.

I know what you're thinking. Spontaneous travel is a pipe dream for the single mom. Not always. Half the time we don't even try to escape because we assume it's impossible. However, I have been pleasantly surprised at my ability to pull off a much-needed weekend away at the very last minute. All it takes is ingenuity, chutzpah, and the ability to beg or bribe with aplomb.

For instance, if you're short on cash, try to work out a weekend trade with another single mom. If she watches your kids this weekend, you'll return the favor. Not only is this better for your children, because with other kids around for the weekend they won't notice your absence as much, it saves you a ton of money on child care as well. And don't forget the relatives. If they're always complaining that they never get to see their grandkids or nieces, tell them you hear them, really you do, so how about a nice long visit *this* weekend? Don't feel bad about doing this once in a while. People are often more than happy to help.

Once you've lined up child care, you're free to go. But where? Sticking close to home is usually best, but you don't want to be so close that you're tempted to turn the car around and head back home because you're feeling guilty. With discount airlines now offering more travel options on short interstate routes, sometimes you can even hop on a plane at the last minute and be in another environment entirely in less than a few hours. (And, as you may recall, airplanes and airports are potential places to meet an eligible guy.)

When you reach your destination, force yourself to have some fun. Window-shop at the overpriced boutiques. Take a golf lesson. Tour the museum. Do *not* sit in the hotel room watching television. You can do that at home. Make friends with the people at the front desk at your hotel. They can make your stay heavenly or hellish, so don't skimp on the tips. And let them know you're alone and looking for some fun and excitement (make sure they don't interpret this to mean you'd like a male prostitute to come knockin' on your door late that night). Hotel employees live in the area. They know the best places to go and things to do, and they are usually delighted to tell you all about it.

Even though millions of women travel alone for business every day, many are still uncomfortable traveling alone for pleasure. However, it's a good habit to get into, as it makes you more self-sufficient and teaches you how to become a savvier travel consumer, which means you'll save time and money over the long haul. The travel industry has started to cater to single women traveling alone. For more information on the services available, see the Additional Resources section at the end of this book.

So, How Long Has It Been?

Have you ever sat around with your single girlfriends and compared notes on when you last had a date? It can turn into the most bizarre kind of one-upmanship: "I haven't had sex for a year," says one. "Oh I can top that. The last time I had a boyfriend, ponytails on guys were still in style," your friend counters. "Two years. I haven't had a decent lay in two years," says another. Okay, you give up, she wins.

What is this fascination with the "dry spell" all about? We're embarrassed yet at the same time perversely proud of how long we can go without love, sex, or male companionship. When I started writing this book nearly two years ago, I was in the middle of one myself. At the time, I realized my son had outgrown two shoe sizes since my last date. Thankfully, his feet tend to grow like watermelon in summertime. But that still means I'd spent at least one summer without any sizzle, and another one was coming up fast.

I could have done the logical thing and put it into perspective: I'd been busy as hell, moving, starting to write this book, and working full-time while at the same time raising twin boys all by myself. No wonder I hadn't had a date.

Still, it made me wonder: if I actually had the time, would I actually have the guys?

Men go through dry spells, too, only they never, ever admit it. Even if their last hot date was while the *first* Bush sat in the Oval Office, he'd have you believing he's a regular lothario.

But not us girls. No, we whine to anyone within earshot about how no one's asking us out, how we couldn't get laid even if we paid, about how we will never date again. I've been guilty of this in the past, but in recent years I've come to accept my dry spells, if only because, as I grow older, there seem to be more and more of them (because, as we grow older, there are fewer available men).

If you find yourself in the middle of the dating desert with no refreshments in site, there are a few things you can do to cope.

- Stay away from stores like IKEA. These places are populated by happy couples focused on feathering their nests, nuzzling each other publicly and tossing glances of pity your way. When you are in the middle of a dry spell, the number of couples in these places seems to multiply, as if by magic, until every direction you turn you see another twosome. Finally, in your own affection-deprived and possibly deranged mind, you will believe *you are the only unattached person in the entire twenty-thousand-square-foot warehouse.* And then suddenly you are so ashamed that you must leave quickly, without that (supposedly) easy-to-assemble media cabinet you've been pining for.

- Get busy—and fast. Pull out your to-do list or hop on a plane.

- Make a list of every guy you've ever slept with. No matter what the number, you'll be comforted by the thought that another guy always came along. Eventually.

Even the longest dry spell will one day come to an end. It just has to. Mine did. And when I finally found my way out of the dating desert and came upon my oasis, I realized that going without love for a long time was really just the universe's way of making me appreciate it more once I'd found it.

It All Adds Up

You are on your way to building a well-rounded life, full of friends, interesting experiences, and a whole new attitude. Piece by piece, every single mom is capable of building a happy, satisfying life for herself and her children. We know what it takes, and we know what we need to do it. Now if the rest of the world could just catch up to us, we'd be all set. As we'll discuss in the next chapter, there's still some work to do on this front, and we can't do it without you, single mom. Let's go.

chapter ten

The Next

Sexual

Revolution

PEACE, LOVE, AND UNDERSTANDING—
HOW SOCIETY CAN HELP OR HINDER
YOUR SEARCH FOR AN IDEAL MATE

"Love and respect woman.
Look to her not only for comfort, but for
strength and inspiration and the doubling of
your intellectual and moral powers.
Blot out from your mind any idea of superiority;
you have none."
—Giuseppe Mazzini, Italian propagandist and founder of
the secret revolutionary society Young Italy

"The thing women have yet to learn is
nobody gives you power. You just take it."
—Roseanne Barr

By now you've probably figured out that love and sex for single moms is a multifaceted affair. Enhancing your inner and outer beauty, learning what you really want in a mate, educating your children about your need for adult companionship—these are just some of the essential ingredients to a happy, fulfilling love life. And succeeding at dating also takes confidence. Thanks to the single mother's rapidly evolving place in society, self-assurance and greater self-esteem are now more easily within reach. But we're not there yet.

Scared Senseless

Have you ever had a romance fall apart for no rational reason, and when you ask your friends what they think happened, they say somberly, "I think maybe you scared him off"? Or maybe the guy himself will tell you later that he bailed on you because he was afraid of you.

When this happens it's hard not to laugh—even though you might be crying. Here you are, a single mother with too much on your plate, not enough money in your bank account, and sometimes low self-esteem. What exactly is so frightening about *you*?

Well, for starters, you are in charge of your own life, whether you wanted to be or not. You are the head of the household. You make your own money, pump your own gas, and take care of your family's needs as best you can. *So what*, you say? Well, as far as some men are concerned, this puts you just one step away from running the free world or, at the very least, their lives. (Guys, get a clue: it's hard enough to run our own.) On an intimate scale, this kind of fear can lead some men to run from what might have been a great relationship. On a grand scale, it can, and has, led to a widespread effort to keep down anyone who might threaten the status quo. In other words, you.

For years, single moms weren't a problem for fans of a patriarchal society. There weren't enough of us to do any harm, and besides, by cutting off educational and professional opportunities and encouraging discrimination and public disdain for our ilk, single moms could easily be kept in their place.

But today, our place is everywhere—in politics, business, the arts, education, you name it—and this freaks out anyone who equates the potential for a more matriarchal society with Armageddon. And trust me, there are a lot of people who do, even though cultural anthropologists have long known that female-headed societies have generally proven to be more peaceful and equitable for all who live there—men included—than patriarchies.

IN REMOTE CHINA, CHICKS RULE

Matriarchal societies have mostly disappeared from the earth, but in southwest China an ethnic minority called the Mosuo still practices the system, making it one of the last true matriarchies on our planet. And when you consider how their social system works, you may be tempted to start your own little matriarchy right here at home.

The Mosuo live in "clan houses" where the mother holds the highest position. They are the head of the household, and in charge of work, financial, and property manners. Mosuo girls live in their own mother's homes all their lives. In addition, each adult Mosuo woman has an *azhu*, or a special house of her own where her lover can visit her during the night—kind of her own little love shack. If the woman decides she's no longer interested in a particular man, she simply "closes the door" to her *azhu*, and he knows he must not return. Talk about your hassle-free breakup.

This is not to say Mosuo women see their lovers as disposable entities; rather, the absence of any legal or economic ties means the relationship is based solely on mutual love and affection, and the wishes of the woman are highly respected. If the relationship results in a pregnancy, the child belongs to the mother's side of the family and inherits her surname. The mother's brothers raise the children along with her, and the kids don't even meet their biological father until an "adult ceremony" later in life. Marriage simply does not exist in traditional Mosuo cultures.

Although this system may sound a bit odd to us, it has endured for centuries for one simple reason: it works. Scholars credit the lack of complex relationships for the absence of conflict among family members. Children, instead of being raised by parents who are in a romantic relationship, are raised by two adults with a blood connection. Some theorize this minimizes conflict between adults and provides more stability and harmony for the kids.

Hell would have to freeze over several times before our society would even consider adopting such practices, but the reality is that there are millions of single mothers who are already reigning over their own little matriarchies. For instance, more and more single moms are choosing to pool their resources and share housing or even buy property together, thanks in great part to the innovative service Co-Abode (www.co-abode.com). And even more single moms are taking control of their romantic lives by choosing how and when they will enjoy sex. Some are shying away from marriage for the same reasons the Mosuo have for generations: it can result in some very messy situations if things don't work out (think custody battles, damaged credit ratings, childhood trauma, or worse).

> Indeed, pretty much the only thing missing from our own little matriarchies is a separate little house just for making love—wouldn't that be nice? Oh, and the fact that most of us no longer live with our mothers—but maybe that's a good thing.

Based on the number of relationship and dating books out there I think it's safe to say that most women are more interested in finding an equal partner than a seat on a throne, but our very independence can sometimes get in the way of reaching this goal. It's a catch-22: to survive, we need to be strong and fend for ourselves. And in doing so, we've found new confidence and reserves of strength and ingenuity we never knew we had. Now that we've had a taste of that self-empowerment, we aren't about to give it back. Yet, we still want love in our lives. Why can't we have both?

You can, if you address some of the factors that can complicate your quest to have it all. These include a number of challenges that have nothing to do with losing weight or joining a singles club. Rather, you should consider where you and your "sisters"—other single moms—fit within today's society, and how that affects your ability to live a full, well-rounded life—one that includes romance.

You have grown tremendously through your experiences as a single parent. It's time to teach others that they need to evolve, too.

Evolution Requires a Revolution

Make no mistake: we are at a pivotal moment in history for single motherhood. We are poised on the cusp of real change, including the possibility for significant improvements to our lives on all fronts. Then again, we are also at the point where all the painful progress we've made over the last several decades could be bombed back to the Stone Age by paranoid politicians and fear-mongering "traditional family" advocates. Which direction we head is ultimately up to the tens of millions of single moms in America and around the world.

Whether your politics lean left or right or sit smack dab in the center, it's important that you realize you're part of a large and growing demographic group. Because at a certain point, all politics is personal—and in your case, getting personal affects your family. No matter how strongly you hold your religious beliefs and moral values, try not to let ideology trump good parenting. True family values—which can be represented by any camp, Republican or Democrat, the religious right or the agnostic left—mean providing equitable social and economic policies. Frankly, I don't care where help for single moms comes from—I just want it to get here, and fast.

By the way, if you feel this kind of commentary has no place in a book about dating and relationships, you haven't been paying attention. Your self-esteem has been fundamental to every piece of advice contained here, and society's treatment of single moms directly affects your self-esteem. We've discussed all the ways your life makes it insanely hard to date and have healthy relationships, so we don't need obstacles put up by the companies that employ us, the courts that preside over us, the media that blares at us day and night, and the policies of our government. So if you really want to find the relationship of your dreams, you need to help create a society where life for single moms isn't such a nightmare.

"I'm a social worker, so I work with many single moms. I always go to bat for them 110 percent because I know personally what it's like. I have been frowned upon and told that my daughter and I aren't a family because it is just us. I think things are better now for single moms than twenty years ago, but we still have a long way to go. The agency I work for knows to tread lightly when talking about single moms. Many people think things are better in other families just because there are two parents. I think single moms need to fight like hell for their rights. I think women in general need to do this, but especially single moms. If there is something they feel strongly about, they should contact their government representative. Speak loud and proud!"

—Kelly, 37, Maine

First, the Good News

It's a great time to be a single mother. Just think how utterly limited your life would be if you were an "unwed mother" or an "abandoned wife" back in the 1950s or '60s. Today, you can accomplish things that single moms of yesteryear could only dream of (and trust me, they did).

Best of all, it seems like single mothers are finally being accepted as, well, normal. There are plenty of individuals and organizations to thank for this, but let's start by giving credit where it's due: to our kids. I don't necessarily mean your own children (although, of course, they're your biggest fan), but rather the youth of today. The generation that is now in their late teens and early twenties are some of the most accepting and forward-thinking people ever. They tend to be more than okay with alternative lifestyles and they strongly support personal freedoms. And since many of them grew up in nontraditional households, thanks to the high divorce rate, they are far less judgmental about women raising children alone.

Consider a study conducted at East Carolina State University, the results of which were published in *College Student Journal* back in 2000, in which university students were asked about their attitudes toward single motherhood. Nearly 80 percent of the respondents agreed that "it is perfectly okay for a woman to decide to have and to raise a child without a husband," with significantly more women (85 percent) than men (73 percent) in agreement. In addition, women were more likely than men to agree that children can develop just as well with *either* a single mother *or* a single father. Finally, women were less likely (26 percent) than men (48 percent) to believe that men are better disciplinarians of children. One can only presume that this level of acceptance of single mothers has only increased in the last several years, especially since even more kids entering college today were raised by single moms.

The sheer number of single moms today means that just about everyone knows at least one of us. And the more they know us, the more they appreciate our efforts to be good parents and just generally good people.

But many single moms aren't waiting around for someone to solve their problems for them—they are finding solutions themselves. Consider women like Carmel Sullivan, founder of Co-Abode.com, who realized that finding safe, suitable housing was one of the biggest hurdles for single mothers and did something about it. Or Dianne Hadaway, the tireless mom behind About.com's single parents website (www.singleparents.about.com), a veritable gold-mine of information on everything from how to handle stress to smart money management. Or civil and women's rights activist Gwen Moore, a single mom who went from being on welfare to becoming the first African-American woman to serve in the Wisconsin state senate. These single moms and countless others are finding unique ways to make life better for us and our families.

A LITTLE RESPECT, PLEASE: SINGLE MOMS THAT CHANGED THE WORLD

History tends to focus on the achievements of men. You know, guys who accomplished amazing feats, like Albert Einstein or George Washington. But I ask you: do you think Einstein would have been able to come up with the theory of relativity if he'd been up all night with a colicky baby? And how could the general have even considered stepping onto a battlefield with a wee one in tow?

The truth is, they wouldn't have. That's why the accomplishments of these single mothers from yesterday and today are so amazing. With the added challenge of raising children alone, they managed to make major contributions to the arts, science, politics, and human rights.

So the next time you're feeling like a second-class citizen, let these myth-shattering single moms inspire you:

GEORGE SAND (1804–76)

Writer, rabble-rouser, and free spirit, she didn't let being a girl stop her from writing some of the greatest literary works ever. She simply used some guy's name as a pseudonym and got to work—while raising two children on her own, having sensational love affairs, and breaking barriers for women all over Europe.

ISADORA DUNCAN (1878–1927)

She revolutionized dance and led a dramatic, if tragedy-filled, life. The suffering she experienced following the death of her two children inspired her art, and she created a legacy that lives on in the dance world today.

MARGARET SANGER (1883–1966)

The mother of the reproductive rights movements, Sanger led the charge to legalize birth control. Without her, you'd have a lot more kids than you do now.

JACKIE KENNEDY ONASSIS (1929–94)

Widow, style icon, loving mother, and classiest first lady ever, she reinvented herself completely after her husband's assassination and led a fascinating life while remaining devoted to her two children.

DIANA, PRINCESS OF WALES (1961–97)

A role model to millions around the world, beautiful, sensitive Diana Spencer endured the marriage from hell and still had the strength to perform important charity works, including a campaign against land mines.

CORETTA SCOTT KING (1927–2006)

The widow of the prominent civil rights activist Dr. Martin Luther King continued her husband's human rights work for decades—and she did so while raising her children alone.

DIANE KEATON (1946–)

An accomplished actress and an inspiration to adoptive single mothers everywhere, Keaton is living proof that growing older can also mean growing better.

Still, There's Plenty to Gripe About

Unfortunately, the growing support for single moms hasn't trickled up as much as it should—namely, to our elected representatives or the people who sign our paychecks. In fact, in the last several years single mothers have suffered some pretty serious setbacks in a number of areas:

- Men still earn more than women for no good reason. On average, women are paid only 76 cents for every dollar a man is paid. The wage gap especially harms women of color: According to the National Organization for Women, an African-American woman receives only 69 cents for every dollar a white male is paid, and a Hispanic woman gets only 56 cents. Families lose an average of $4,000 each year due to the wage gap; over the course of her career, the average woman loses about $250,000 due to sex discrimination in pay.

- Tax cuts for the wealthy hurt single moms more than any other demographic. A 2004 issue of the *National NOW Times*, published by the National Organization for Women, stated, "A fundamental change of the Bush II era shifted more of the tax burden from upper income brackets onto the middle class, while providing little or no relief for the lowest income earners, according to a recent Congressional Budget Office report. More than seven million families with incomes between $10,500 and $26,500 did not receive the 2003 increase in the child tax credit, disproportionately affecting single women raising children."

- The recently passed Bankruptcy Bill means it's harder to get a fresh start after a divorce or to get child support that is owed. Single mothers, who often work in low-wage jobs, are 50 percent more likely to file for bankruptcy than married parents, and three times more likely than childless couples, according to an article published in the *Christian Science Monitor*. In 2005, the *Workers Independent News* warned that "The new law wipes out the priority status that back child support has and instead puts single moms on equal footing with credit card collection agencies as they try to get paid in a bankruptcy."

This list could go on for some time, which is pretty depressing. So instead of getting down about it, let's make a list of all the things we would change if we could cast a magic spell. Essentially, we'll create what I call a single mom manifesto. Many of the following items came from single mothers I corresponded with during the creation of this book. Note: if you're not sure how to cast a magic spell, see the Additional Resources section of this book for ways you can get involved.

Single Mom Manifesto

Nearly every single mom I heard from mentioned many of the same obstacles to eliminating stress in their lives. On the face of it, these problems seem entirely solvable. We're not asking for much. But in order to make progress on these issues, we need to speak louder, because obviously people aren't listening. Here are a few things to shout about:

- Fixing the wage gap
- Providing affordable health insurance for kids and families
- Ending housing and job discrimination against single mothers
- Providing more flexible work schedules
- Creating low- or no-cost child-care solutions
- Treating us with respect and consideration

What about a Men-ifesto?

Changing the world is one thing, but right now you're probably more interested in finding a great guy to go to the movies with. Creating a list can help you here as well; it should include the things you absolutely cannot live without, as well as the attributes you'd *like* to have in a partner but won't insist upon. Here are some traits to think about as you make your own men-ifesto:

- Age
- Parenting experience

- Religious or spiritual orientation

- Level of education

- Political point of view

- Penis size (I'm only half-joking)

- Sense of humor

- Financial stability

- Emotional stability

- Grooming and manners

- Social skills

The idea here is to have a strong sense of what you want in a mate so you don't waste your time on guys who meet only one of your criteria, like, say, penis size or eye color. I heard from some single moms who, in order to avoid repeating their mistakes, developed a pretty firm grasp on what they do and do not want— and, more importantly, *why* they simply won't settle for less. Here are a couple of men-ifestos that really hit home for me:

"Understand that my kid comes first, always. He's only two and there is no way I am going to deny him his mother for anything but extremely good reasons (like having to make a living)— especially since he doesn't get to spend every day with me. Someone I'm dating will always come after kid and income-producing activities.

Understand that my child does not need a father, nor am I looking for someone to be his father—he has one who is very devoted to him. Attempts to discipline or 'parent' my kid will not be welcome.

Understand that I like my life the way it is now! And that I do *not* need a man to feel happy and complete. I am not looking to be rescued or relieved of anything.

Understand that I may need to cancel or change plans at the last minute. Understand that I cannot be spontaneous. Understand that parenting right takes up a lot of time, and that because I have to be away from him a lot, when I am able to, I often just want to be alone with my son rather than with you (or anyone else). Understand that you are going to need to work with my schedule, rather than fit me into yours."

—Christine, 37, New York City

"Love my kid, but don't try to be his dad. Don't treat me like Ms. All-Powerful-I-Am-So-Capable-I-Do-It-All-By-Myself. I'm still a woman. I still get PMS and eye expensive jewelry and am still wowed by little romantic gestures like flowers and chocolates.

Don't flaunt your unrestricted, no-kids-holding-me-down, I'll-go-out-every-night-and-tell-you-all-about-it life. You think I don't see it? Maybe just once skip drinking with the guys to stay in with me while the baby sleeps."

—Julie, 21, Boston

"The attributes a man must possess to be involved in my life, on any level, are very specific and non-negotiable. First and foremost he must have a clear understanding of the value that I place on my time. Boundaries must be clear, and he must not be needy on any level. He must understand if I don't call him for days, it's not because I am not interested, or that I am angry, just that I am busy.

He must respect me as a mother and not only remember but also acknowledge the fact that my children are my family, not his. That's not to say that I am unwilling to share my children; just that I am the ultimate authority on them. I do not want his ideas, morals, and values forced upon my children, nor do I not want him disciplining them any more than simply saying no. He must understand that although he is important to me, and he does add value and enrichment to my life, my life is my children. They will always be the most important thing to me. No one will ever rate above my children; his needs will always be second to those of my children. Therefore, he must be self-confident and resourceful. He can't rely on me to constantly build up his ego; I don't have the time, the energy, or the inclination to do such a thing. He must treat my children with the utmost love and respect, even if they do not earn it. All of this said, he must also be willing to help me when I am overburdened or in a time of distress. He must not pass judgment on me or question the way that I am raising my children. And he must be very, very funny because I love to laugh.

Are you still wondering why I am single?"

—Lucy, 29, Seattle

And What about Single Dads?

In the last few years single fathers have become much more organized as a special interest group. Organizations intended to fight for fathers' visitation rights, for example, have received a lot of attention. And while the majority of single-parent households in this country are headed by women, there are plenty of single fathers out there, and they struggle with many of the same issues we do—with one critical exception: single fathers tend to be admired, rather than denigrated, for their situation. Oh, and members of the opposite sex often find a man's status as a single parent sexy rather than a turnoff.

Other than that, the challenges that single mothers and single fathers face are amazingly similar. I heard from one such dad, and I've excerpted his story here:

"People hold me in high respect for the course I have taken and the challenge that I stare in the face. Strangers see single moms or hear a single mom's story every day and never give it a second thought because it is so common. Strangers see me or hear my story and, without fail, people tell me how proud they are of me, how good it is to see a single father raising his children alone, taking the initiative and doing what's best for the kids. I have earned a lot of respect from everyone I know and even people I don't know.

I am a pretty young guy to have such a load on my plate, but I wouldn't have it any other way, and I would do it all over again the same way. All my friends are out partying, living it up. They always tell me, "I don't know how you do it, man. I have a lot of respect for you!" And that makes me feel good.

Some women see a guy with his children and think "Aw, how cute is that?" And I admit, I have been approached several times just because I had the kids with me. It really depends on the girl. Some girls see that and think to themselves "Father, loves kids, good guy, has custody, shows stability," and that attracts them.

Others may see the same guy and think "baggage!" Then there is always the "ex-factor." The ex-wife is going to be around until the kids are eighteen, minimum. There is a lot of understanding and patience that has to go along with dating a single parent. So all in all, I think single parents have a disadvantage when it comes to the dating scene. It's not uncommon to plan a date, then something comes up and you can't make it. The sitter may cancel, or their mom may have to go to work, or one of the kids might be sick or have to go to a school function—it could be many different things.

I think the person I would date would have to like kids or even have children of her own. You cannot expect to have a decent relationship with someone when you are a single parent and the other person is not fond of children. Also, patience and understanding is *huge.* The other person is going to have to accept that things just don't work out as planned most of the time when there are children involved. Also, I want someone who has enough respect that they would never in a million years put you in a position where you have to choose between them and time with your children. They will always lose. If someone asks you to do something and you respond with "I can't, it's my weekend with my children," they shouldn't have the audacity to say, "So? Just get a sitter!" That is *not* cool. When you're a single parent, your standards should be elevated to the point where it is almost impossible to find someone to date.

You have to be a strong individual to cope with the daily pressures of trying to make a living and raising children. You have to possess patience, love, understanding, and compassion, all the while keeping in mind that you are leading by example every single minute of every single day. I have three sets of eyes on me at all times, whether I know it or not. They are always watching, learning, picking up habits, good or bad.

Heaven to me is just me and the kids. Living without negative outside influences (i.e., their mother), I have been allowed the opportunity to be the father I wanted to be. When I was married, most of the time I was too upset with their mother to enjoy them. Now that it's just the kids and me, we make the best of our time together.

I would be just fine with watching my kids grow up and become successful and being single the whole time. But if that certain someone comes along and exceeds all the expectations I have set forth for the next woman in my life, then the more the merrier."

—Mark, 29, Dallas

"Single dads make the best dates."

—Susan, 34, Kentucky

It's up to You

I saw a great bumper sticker the other day. It read, "Quit bitchin' and start a revolution." If change for you begins by altering your approach to love and romance, that's great. If you're inclined to take a broader approach to making life for single moms better, such as by getting active in your community or taking part in a support group, that's great, too.

Either way, your future—and your children's future—is in your hands. By believing in yourself and all you have to offer a romantic partner and the world at large, you can make your life as a single mom one that others will admire and perhaps even envy. Based upon the stories I heard from single mothers of varying ages, locations, ethnicities, and income levels, my sense is that in general, you're doing pretty well despite the tremendous hurdles you face. Damn good, in fact. Sure, some days are really, really tough, and sometimes you're lonely, but you're working on fixing that. You're reading this book for one thing, and you're deciding not to settle for anything but the best in all aspects of your life. In short, there's nothing holding you back.

Let your revolution begin.

> *"I love being a single mom. If I meet someone, that will be great and if I don't, then that's okay, too. So many people say, 'I don't know how you do it alone.' Truthfully, I do not know how to do it any other way."*
>
> *—Kelly, 37, Maine*

resources

Single Parenthood

BOOKS

The Complete Single Mother by Andrea Engber and Leah Klungness (Adams Media Corporation)

> A thorough, resource-rich guide for women new to single motherhood.

Four Weeks to a Better Behaved Child by Christine Chandler with Laura McGrath (McGraw-Hill)

> Unique tactics and advice for discipline-challenged parents.

Marriage, A History: From Obedience to Intimacy or How Love Conquered Marriage by Stephanie Coontz (Viking)

> The author takes a good, long look at marriage from ancient times to today and discovers that love has often been missing from the institution. A great book that's especially interesting for anyone considering remarriage.

The Mommy Myth: The Idealization of Motherhood and How It Has Undermined Women by Susan Douglas and Meredith Michaels (The Free Press)

> This book has made quite a ruckus, and for good reason: It blows some mighty big holes in the myths surrounding society's images of motherhood.

Operating Instructions: A Journal of My Son's First Year by Anne Lamott (Ballantine Books)

> Perhaps the funniest, most honest account of experiencing pregnancy and a baby's first year as a single mom.

The Single Mother's Survival Guide by Patrice Karst (The Crossing Press)

> An easy, uplifting read that goes a long way toward helping single moms feel better about the many challenges in their lives.

WEBSITES

Insanity House: www.insanityhouse.com

> A wonderful community for single mothers working for social, economic, and political change.

My very own website: www.sexandthesinglemom.com

> Give me feedback on the book, join our community, and even do a little shopping. Please stop by and say hello.

Single Mother Resources: www.singlemotherresources.com

> This site focuses heavily on the financial challenges faced by single mothers and offers information on scholarships, debt management, and related topics.

Single Parent Central: www.singleparentcentral.com

> A friendly and wide-ranging site for single parents, with articles, links, and useful information on topics from child care subsidies to how to avoid work-at-home scams.

About.com's single parent website: www.singleparents.about.com

> Under the careful guidance of Dianne Hadaway, this site provides timely and wide-ranging information for single parents, much of it centered around holidays or important dates (back to school, Christmas without your kids, and so on) and on specific themes such as managing your finances.

True's magazine for single parents: www.true.com/magazine/sparent_
main.htm
> A small but lively group of articles and research findings of particu-
> lar interest to single parents.

GROUPS

Single Moms by Choice: http://groups.yahoo.com/group/singlemomby
choice
> This is a friendship and support group hosted on Yahoo Groups.
> Women who are single moms by choice often have unique needs and
> concerns. This group also welcomes women who are thinking about
> becoming (or trying to become) single mothers by choice. Note that
> this group is not for single mothers with partners in the picture.

Parents without Partners: www.parentswithoutpartners.org
> This nonprofit group is one of the oldest single-parent support
> organizations. With more than two hundred chapters in the United
> States and Canada, they focus on educational, social, and recreational
> activities for single parents and their families.

National Organization of Single Mothers: www.singlemothers.org
> Founded in 1991, this advocacy group for single mothers conducts
> research and reaches out to the media on issues of concern to single
> mothers.

Dating and Relationships

BOOKS

*He's Just Not That into You: The No-Excuses Truth to Understanding
Guys* by Greg Behrendt and Liz Tuccillo (Simon Spotlight Entertainment)
> This book contains some harsh truths about men and the excuses
> they make, but as the saying goes, the truth will set you free. It's also
> a fun, fast, and ultimately helpful guide.

If the Buddha Dated by Charlotte Kasl (Penguin)
> The author applies Buddhist principles to the very un-Zen process
> of modern-day dating. The result is an uplifting spiritual guide to
> love and relationships.

The Improvised Woman: Single Women Reinventing Single Life by Mar-
celle Clemens (W.W. Norton and Company)
> I read this book again and again before I became a single mom, and
> find it even more relevant now. One of the first books that dares to
> suggest that women can lead fulfilling lives without a man at the cen-
> ter of it.

Red Flags: How to Know When You're Dating a Loser by Gary Aumiller
and Daniel Goldfarb (Plume)
> Two psychologists describe the various types of losers women should
> be wary of: liars, know-it-alls, cheaters, and other lower life forms.
> Recognize the warning signs before it's too late.

Sex and the Single Girl by Helen Gurley Brown (Barricade Books)
> A groundbreaking book when it was first published decades ago.
> Much of the advice still rings true today.

WEBSITES

A great blog about Internet dating: http://e-dating.blogspot.com/
> A roundup of news and helpful articles about Internet dating and
> relationships in general.

Online dating: www.lavalife.com
> This Canadian-based online dating service brands itself as sexy and
> entertaining. The company has grown exponentially since its launch.
> It even features international versions so you can connect with sin-
> gles around the world in your own language.

Dating site for socially conscious singles: www.realidate.com

> The premise behind this service is to match people who are into vol-
> unteering, charitable giving, or environmental activism. Kind of like
> a Sierra Club mixer without the five-mile hike before lunch.

Single Parent Love Life: www.singleparentlovelife.com

> This is the first dating site that caters to and understands the unique
> realities of single parents. Profile and search preferences are tailored
> to the situations that single parents deal with every day. It is a much-
> needed alternative to the one-size-fits-all approach of the main-
> stream dating sites, and also invites the millions of "singles open to
> meeting single parents" to join the service.

True relationship matching: www.true.com

> This online dating service features criminal-background screening
> and promises to prosecute married people posing as available singles.
> Members complete a scientific compatibility test to help them find
> the appropriate matches.

Sex, Beauty, and Health

BOOKS

Advanced Sex Tips for Girls: This Time It's Personal by Cynthia Heimel
(Simon and Schuster)

> More of the same funny stuff, but updated.

Everything You Know About Love and Sex is Wrong by Dr. Pepper
Schwartz (Perigree Trade)

> Dr. Schwartz skewers the heavily ingrained assumptions that often
> doom our relationships and lead to dull sex lives.

The Happy Hook-Up: A Single Girl's Guide to Casual Sex by Alexa Joy
Sherman and Nicole Tocantins (Ten Speed Press)

> A sassy, no-guilt guide to sex without commitment.

Sex Tips for Girls by Cynthia Heimel (Fireside)
> This book has been passed between my girlfriends for as long as I can remember. Hilarious and honest, it's required reading for any woman with a libido and a sense of humor.

The Truth about Beauty: Transform Your Looks and Your Life from the Inside Out by Kat James (Beyond Words Publishing)
> James's philosophy is a unique blend of natural treatments, the enhancement of your inner beauty, and the importance of eating the right foods.

Vaginas: An Owner's Manual by Elizabeth Topp and Dr. Carol Livoti (Thunder's Mouth Press)
> There's more to a healthy, happy vagina than you might think. With wit and style, Dr. Livoti and her daughter take on the myths surrounding this part of our anatomy, while providing important information about STDs and common disorders of the vagina, uterus, and surrounding equipment. In between, they wisecrack plenty.

YOU, The Owner's Manual: An Insider's Guide to the Body That Will Make You Healthier and Younger by Michael Roizen and Mehmet Oz (Collins)
> The best thing about this book is that you don't need a medical degree to figure out what's going on with your body. It doesn't cover everything, particularly for women, but it offers an easy introduction to how our bodies work, and what happens when they don't.

WEBSITES

An index of links to health and beauty sites: www.carejournal.org
> A list of links to just about every health and beauty topic you could ever imagine.

Reliable information about STDs: www.mayoclinic.com
> When something just doesn't feel right down there, go here before you panic and start calling all your girlfriends. This site is the most

reliable, well-organized, and up-to-date resource for all health issues, including those of a sexual nature.

A digital magazine about sex: www.nerve.com

It took a lot of nerve to launch this site some years back, and it's still going strong. From articles on sex for new parents to reviews of the latest reality television shows, Nerve covers it all with aplomb.

Life
(jobs, housing, networking, activism, travel, socializing, and other cool stuff)

Reconnect with people from your past: www.classmates.com

Single moms will be delighted to know they are not the only ones from their high school who are currently unattached. And, who knows, that cute guy you had a crush on in ninth grade could be a member.

Single mother housing match service: www.co-abode.com

A wonderful service that matches single moms in need of housing. Because of this site, many single moms have made lifelong friendships and saved a bunch of money on housing.

Classifieds, community, pretty much everything: www.craigslist.org

Whether you want to sell your crib or your car, join a single mom's group, start a rock band, or simply get a new job, Craigslist is the place to go. Fans of this no-frills site are loyal, fanatical even, because it works—and it's free.

Events, activities, and more for families: www.gocitykids.com

When Saturday comes and you're fresh out of ideas for keeping the kids entertained, go to Go City Kids. They have up-to-date calendars for events and activities in your area, many of which are no-cost or low-cost.

Inside dirt on Washington politics: www.huffingtonpost.com
This website shares breaking news from Washington via a fantastic blog by the smart, sexy, and outspoken Arianna Huffington. It contains some of the best and well-written commentary on the Internet.

Women's rights and activism: www.now.org
The National Organization for Women (NOW) continues to push for the rights of women in all areas of life, from equal pay to job discrimination and then some. If you're enraged or just plain concerned about the state of things for single moms today, see what NOW has to say about it, and get involved.

Travel ideas and tips for single parents: www.singleparenttravel.net
If you're dreading a six-hour plane ride alone with the kids, look into group travel activities with other single parents. Or just check out this site's roundup of discount travel ideas.

Working Mother magazine (print and web): www.workingmother.com
While not particularly focused on the issues of single moms, this can be a good resource for women trying to balance work and family.

index